# Reimagination Station:
# Creating a Game-Changing
# In-Home Coworking Space

by
Lori Kane

Published by Lori Kane

Cover art by: Tabitha Borchardt
Back cover art by Bas de Baar

ISBN-10: 0986299634
ISBN-13: 978-0-9862996-3-6

Lori Kane
www.collectiveself.com
Email: lori@collectiveself.com
Twitter: @collectiveself

Share feedback on the book at:
feedback@collectiveself.com

Printed by Createspace An Amazon.com company

For

Seattle,

the Central District,

Collective Self Coworking,

and our neighbors

# About the Book

What does it mean to reimagine part of your private home as a community space? What does it take to imagine, run, work in, let go of, and play in a free in-home coworking space? What are the impacts of doing so on the homeowners, housemates/renters, neighbors, coworkers, neighborhood, city, and region? We are living answers to these questions and offer experience-based hints for others playing with similar ideas.

This is also a flash non-fiction book that contains found-object art and community-surfaced stories and ideas. We got the idea for the book during coworking on February 4, 2015. We created the book in four weeks—finished March 5th as hoped. We self-published in March to be timely, useful, and affordable for people we love. Friends and neighbors mentioned in community stories can pick up their free copy of the book at the house during coworking in 2015, starting in April.

Feel free to ask me anything about turning our home into community space, about this and other neighborhood reimagination stations we're connected to now, or about the process of creating flash non-fiction and lived-adventure books. Bring your own plan to get me to shut up when you need to go. In person, about subjects I love, I do tend to go on a bit.

– Lori

lori@collectiveself.com

# Contents

My neighborhood roots ..................................................................................... 1

Imagining the Space ...................................................................................... 5

    Hint 1: Fail your ass off. Make one friend in the process. ........................... 6

    Hint 2: Fail your ass off together. Make a few more friends in the process ................ 7

    Hint 3: Notice what you do regularly, without fail. And notice what you're longing for. .............................................................................................................. 8

    Hint 4: Feel your a-ha! moment in your bones. .......................................... 9

    Hint 5: Watch your energy skyrocket at the idea. ..................................... 10

    Hint 6: Imagine just three people in the space as enough. ...................... 11

    Hint 7: Receive input and support from those you share the home with ............... 12

    Hint 8: Receive input and support from neighbors. ................................. 13

    Hint 9: Imagine the space as a gift by neighbors for neighbors. ............. 14

    Hint 10: Accept help with imagination from kind strangers. .................. 15

    Hint 11: Don't imagine the space. .............................................................. 16

Running the Space ....................................................................................... 17

    Hint 12: Show up, unlock the door, take out the trash, and clean the bathroom ..... 18

    Hint 13: Don't run the space. .................................................................... 19

    Hint 14: Connect with other people learning in the same direction online. ........... 20

    Hint 15: Connect with other people learning in the same direction locally. .......... 21

    Hint 16: Imagine the whole space as one big experiment and small pilot ideas. .... 22

    Hint 17: Play. .............................................................................................. 23

    Hint 18: Reimagine yourself as often as you'd like. ................................. 24

    Hint 19: Reimagine relationship building and spreading the word. ........... 26

    Hint 20: Say "Yes!" to people who want to host after-hours events in the space. ..... 28

    Hint 21: Become friends with people in other coworking and collaborative spaces in your area ............................................................................................. 30

    Hint 22: Deep welcome doesn't begin at your door, it begins on the sidewalk and in the street ............................................................................................... 32

    IIint 23: Embrace both welcome and unwelcome as part of your routine now. ....... 33

    Hint 24: Practice running the space with full presence and without words. .......... 35

    Hint 25: Put leadership in its place. ........................................................... 36

    Hint 26: Offer outside-your-comfort-zone alternatives to your space. .......... 37

    Hint 27: Reimagine security and safety. ................................................... 38

    Hint 28: Notice that listening to what is needed by everyone has become a habit. . 41

    Hint 29: Notice that you've turned learning about neighborhood history into a habit. 42

Hint 30: Be prepared for magic...........................................................................43

Hint 31: Field trips!.......................................................................................44

Hint 32: When enough people aren't showing up, grow closer to those who do show up. ......................................................................................................................45

Hint 33: Protect the crap out of your time (aka, learning to say no to dear friends).46

Hint 34: Expect to begin standing up for your neighborhood. A lot.......................47

Hint 35: Fall in love with neighborhood sounds. Change the sounds nobody can live with. ...............................................................................................................48

Hint 36: Expect to become someone new. ........................................................49

Hint 37: Did I mention magic? Let's mention it again, shall we? .......................50

Working in the Space ........................................................................................51

Hint 38: Be a bit fluid with your personal space and personal plans ...................52

Hint 39: If you have specific needs for the day, tell people what your needs are for that day. ..........................................................................................................53

Hint 40: If our space doesn't work for you, before you go, ask about other options.54

Hint 41: Try leading with "How can I contribute?" .........................................55

Hint 42: If you stay, prepare to be wow'd. And loved. ......................................56

Hint 43: Prepare to be needed..........................................................................57

Hint 44: Notice your impact on others. ............................................................58

Hint 45: Don't apologize for being yourself. Don't ask others to either.................59

Hint 46: If you feel unsafe, do something immediately. ......................................60

Hint 47: When uncomfortable, reflect on why you think being uncomfortable is a bad thing. .........................................................................................................61

Hint 48: Don't work in the space. .....................................................................62

Letting Go of the Space......................................................................................63

Hint 49: Notice a shift in your energy. .............................................................64

Hint 50: Do nothing for a while........................................................................65

Hint 51: Watch your energy skyrocket and shift back to your individual/family needs....................................................................................................................66

Hint 52: This time notice that you trust your a-ha! moment implicitly. ..............67

Hint 53: Say "HELL Yes!" to community help. Witness magic............................68

Hint 54: Let go with minimal sadness. You carry the space inside you now. ..........69

Hint 55: Revel in being your more whole weird self—not the visible leader...........70

Hint 56: Don't let go of the space......................................................................72

Hint 57: If handing off the space to someone else, tell them three things about running the space, then stop..........................................................................................73

Who's That Playing in the Space Between? ........................................................75

Hint 58: Embracing the stranger in yourself......................................................76

Hint 59: Keeping a kind stranger generator in your basement. In case of emergency. 77

Hint 60: Bowing in deep gratitude for this life. ...........................................................78

Hint -11,385.1a: Embracing the quirky weirdo in yourself.......................................79

Hint 62: Playing together to remember all life as a gift we receive. ..........................80

Hint 63: Happening upon beauty and fun everywhere. ..............................................81

Hint 64: Watching life for deep words, community stories, and little reminders. ...82

Hint 65: Experiencing connections within and across stories....................................84

Hint 66: Living beyond conventional (for you) ideas, expectations, and roles. .......85

Hint 67: Letting go of planning...................................................................................87

Hint 68: Shattering......................................................................................................88

Hint 69: Taking my name and titles off my business cards and losing them entirely.90

Hint 70: Moving like the wind. ...................................................................................91

Hint 71: Falling deeply in love with space and place and people. ..............................92

Hint 72: Recognizing the space between as home, too. ..............................................93

Hint 73: Accepting the child's gift: deep imagination. ..............................................94

Epilogue: my neighborhood wings...............................................................................95

Community Mementos..................................................................................................97

About the Lived-Adventure Series ............................................................................ 103

About the Author.......................................................................................................104

About the Cover Illustrators .....................................................................................105

# My neighborhood roots

This wandering girl fell in love with the Central District at age 26. It was 1996 and I'd been living in Greenwood and driving to Pill Hill two nights a week as a volunteer English-as-a-second-language tutor for St. James' language program for immigrants and refugees. I couldn't afford world travel—I couldn't even afford outside-the-city travel—so spending time with people from all parts of the world at St. James was as close as I was going to get.

For two years I drove my friend and favorite student Belit home at night to her Central District home, even though it was against policy for volunteers to drive students home. We were such rebels. Belit's from Ethiopia. Her husband Gebrahan is from Eritrea. Six of their 8 kids still lived at home with them. To an outsider, Belit and I must have looked ridiculous together at times—me, taught to honor my elders above all else, always deferring to her. And her, a woman who had never been inside a school in her 44 years, taught to honor teachers above all else, always deferring to me. It's amazing we got anything done at all.

We bonded quickly over our unlikely shared history in South Dakota—the place where I'd grown up and the place they'd spent their first 6 months in the U.S. after fleeing civil war. They'd never seen thick snow and ice on the ground, and tall Gebrahan landed flat on his back the first time he'd walked across it. One of their favorite South Dakota stories—and mine—was from the night Belit went into labor with their youngest son. It was two in the morning, they spoke almost no English, they were brand new dark-skinned strangers in a strange freezing-cold white land, and they needed immediate help. The only English Gebrahan could say as he pounded on their neighbors' doors in the middle of the night was "Baby coming! Baby coming!" which, as it happily turned out, brought them all the help they needed. Brought out people who treated them like family. So they'd deemed South Dakota very dangerous, because of ice and snow, but with wide open skies and great people, like home. When they learned I was a single young woman from South Dakota, with no family in the Northwest, they took me in instantly. Made me family without a thought. We were strangers no more.

Many of their stories didn't have happy endings. Government officials draining bank accounts and taking land, cars, and homes. Trying to educate children in crowded refugee camps. The women wearing the family's wealth around their necks in gold as they left familiar country after country. At home, they'd been relatively wealthy financially. By the time they got to Seattle, they were relatively financially poor. They beamed with love when speaking of or looking at each other though, so they weren't actually poor. Their older kids, raised in Africa, had a quiet presence that made them seem far older than teenagers. They were fluidly helpful to their folks and beyond thoughtful toward all human beings: "Dark blue suits you, Lori, you are glowing today." Their two youngest kids, raised here in a U.S. city, were fast-talking, sassy, and funny as hell: "Girl, who dressed you today? You look like a nun." These new siblings of mine sounded more like my own little sister three states away. Fashion's never been my strong suit.

My first Central District family wasn't poor: they just didn't have much money. They taught me to make injera. To eat spicy food. To eat popcorn with coffee so intense it gave me an instant headache the first time I tried it. They invited my visiting parents to Easter brunch, where Gebrahan convinced my dad that it was ok for men to share a beer in the morning since "It's just *light* beer." Out of the corner of my eye, I watched my dad begin protesting, decide he'd just found a new loophole for drinking beer whenever he felt like it, and embrace that beyond-generous shared Coors Light with a wide smile. I helped out by teaching Belit practical English for grocery shopping and dealing with plumbers and landlords and salespeople, by reading notes from school that their fast-learning kids could read but they couldn't yet, and by helping with homework, taxes, and gardening in a still-strange land. Belit always walked with me to my car as I left and waved to me until I was out of sight: exactly the way my Grandma Kane on the farm in South Dakota did. Both taught me about the gift of presence and place without ever saying a word. The Central District had my heart.

Two years passed. When I went back to school for a master's degree in Adult Education & Training, I chose Seattle University in large part because of my time with Belit and her family. And by the time I finished at SU, I was working at Microsoft and could afford the neighborhood, so I decided to move to the neighborhood that had treated me like family. In 2002, I bought the home that would one day become Collective Self Coworking. My boyfriend Daniel moved in, housemates moved in, and dogs and cats moved in.

Ten years passed. Daniel and I got married, housemates came and went, and I was busy working at Microsoft, getting a doctorate degree at SU, volunteering in community gardens, and creating our yard from the ground up. Eventually I began working at home as a researcher and blogger. But something was missing. I didn't feel connected to the neighborhood like I'd felt connected back when I was part of Belit's family. I felt stuck on the surface of the neighborhood most days—not going deeper. Which made me feel lost, even in my own home.

In February 2012, our household went with my then-crazy notion to turn our home at 21st and Union into a free community coworking space on Wednesdays. The people of the Central District (and beyond) who showed up reimagined the home even further as community space by adding, for example, Saturday crafternoons and group BBQs. By adding morning parents' meetings and evening impact-of-gentrification salons. By adding event planning meetings and hosting film festivals. They added taking coworking outside to do community gardening, take field trips together, and to help create Hopscotch CD: a now annual neighborhood-wide event. The space changed my whole world by allowing me to slow down, play more, connect deeply with neighbors, and fall deeply in love with our home, our neighbors, my work, our neighborhood, and eventually the whole city again. The space surfaced other grassroots community revealers/builders/dreamers/story wranglers/artists/poets all over the place too—people who've become my own dear friends. The space and the neighborhood, together, taught me to listen more deeply, even told me when it was my time to go.

It's been more than three years now, and Collective Self Coworking continues to be reimagined and used by friends and neighbors. Daniel and I no longer live in the home and I no longer run coworking—others do, although I sometimes come back to host a day for the pure magic of it. I continue to show up to play and work with friends in the CD several times a month. And I connect and support the efforts of our friends across the neighborhood. We learned from friends Derryl and Sharon—long-time CD residents and business owners who moved to Beacon Hill: you don't just walk away from that much awesome. You carry the CD with you, inside you. You go back. You give back. How do you say thank you to a place and a space and the people who quell your fears and allow you to completely reimagine yourself again and again? There are no words.

I love you guys.

- Lori
February 4, 2015
written at Collective Self Coworking in the Central District, Seattle, WA
lori@collectiveself.com

# Collective Self, the Central District's free coworking space, as we looked in 2012

# Imagining the Space

## Hint 1: Fail your ass off. Make one friend in the process.

It was October 2009. I'd worked as a researcher and blogger from our home at 21st and Union for four years, and my romantic notions about working alone at home had long faded. I loved my work, yes, and...

I was lonely. I was forgetting to shower for more days than I have yet to admit to anyone. I stopped liking to go out. At some point the dog, cats, yard, books, Internet, and TV became more enticing than leaving the house to engage with other humans.

Eventually, my aloneness began to impact my work. When I went to sit with people to listen to their stories—a deep love of mine—sometimes it had been so long since I'd spoken out loud to strangers that I came across as stilted and snobby or spacey and unsure of myself in person—none of which was actually true for me most days. I'd gotten so far out of practice at speaking out loud that I was getting rusty at simple conversation.

I tried to establish a regular routine that got me out of the house and working elsewhere. I tried several libraries, countless coffee shops, a few parks, and one of the formal coworking spaces in the city. All were great. And none helped me establish the routine I wanted. I wasn't actually talking to other people in those spaces. I'd learn the names of the dogs in other spaces and always remember to greet the dogs. But I'd forget people names. I'd hole up and speak to no one but the dogs. And I was paying good money for this. Eventually I decided just to talk to my own dog at home and imagine she was talking back to me. It was cheaper.

Next, I tried joining several different writing groups, because I love writing so I should love hanging out with writers, right? For me, not so much back then. I was never compelled to attend any writer's group beyond the first time.

In January 2010, I tried forming my own Meetup discussion group around the subject Fostering the Emergence of Self-Organizing Work Groups, the subject of my doctoral dissertation (and really the only thing I was interested in talking about for several years—ask poor Daniel). The group was wildly popular on paper. More than 20 people signed up to attend immediately. In practice, it sucked. Only two or three people ever came to a gathering. There were also problems with the coffee shops I'd arranged to meet in, such as other people not honoring the sign-up sheet for the mini-conference room I'd reserved. Or people not being able to find us in the library's semi-hidden conference room. The logistics were taking far too much time for me. I just wanted to be together. I didn't want to arrange it.

On the up side, one person came to those discussions every single time. She even began helping with logistics and scheduling. That person was Diane. I love Diane. I'd made one friend! Success!

Hint 2: Fail your ass off together. Make a few more friends in the process.

By summer 2010, Diane and I dumped the group idea and name I'd started with (see story in Hint 1) and reimagined our fledgling group as the Seattle Consultant's Grotto. The name was Diane's idea and I loved it, thinking to myself "Really, the word Consultant is so blah/yuck that it needs a cool partner word like Grotto to sound even remotely interesting." Hello foreshadowing.

We Grotto-ites met monthly and were together almost two years. We managed to have a fluctuating-yet-steady membership of roughly 10 people and to get 4 to 5 people to most monthly meetings. And it was fun. We often met at the Starbucks on 23rd and Jackson—a place where vibrant neighborhood energy collects and expands. There is no separate conference room space like in Starbucks in white neighborhoods. Here, everyone is in it together. Thank God.

I never stopped writing/blogging the whole time I was figuring out how to become a consultant. Eventually, the group helped me figure out that I didn't want to be a consultant at all. I learned this mostly by watching the energy and joy others found working as consultants for large and small organizations. It was so much fun to watch them. And terrifying to realize that the path I'd planned for myself (the one that involved making a living with the expensive degree I'd just earned) was not going to be the path for me after all. Damn. I wrote a short book with another group member, Doug, and realized that co-creating a book was pure joy. When I realized I wasn't a consultant, I talked to the group about it, and left the group.

In the process, I found six people I consider to be life-long friends (love you Tim, Diane, Doug, Cathy, Neil, and Rowena). People I care about no matter where we all go or what we all do or how much time goes by.

Hint 3: Notice what you do regularly, without fail. And notice what you're longing for.

Before I got the idea for the coworking space, and after I figured out I didn't want to be an organizational consultant, I continued to flail about trying to figure out what to do with my life. Because it had worked for me in the past, I did *The Artist's Way* morning pages thingy (write 3 pages in a journal every morning, stream of consciousness, no stopping, no editing. every few weeks, go back and highlight "insights" in one color and "actions" in another color. do this until you move through the block and don't need to do it anymore.)

I came away understanding that:

- I love writing—even the down sides—and I won't ever stop. So I might as well make a living at it or die happily and trying. I still remember the day I told spouse Daniel that I intended to be a writer no matter what. Even if I never got paid and had to live homeless and writing in the dirt it would be well worth it. That was a frickin' fantastic day! For me at least. ;-)

- I was longing for deeper, lasting connections with my neighbors and the community we lived in.

My process isn't important, except to me. Get there how you get there. The important thing here is the deep noticing of what matters most to you.

I still didn't know what to do to make deeper connections in the community I was in. Everybody around me appeared to be far too busy to make and sustain deeper connections with me.

I watched my neighbors with kids make deep connections through their kids' schools.

I watched my religious neighbors use church, temple, or mosque to make those deep connections.

My day-job friends and neighbors made deep connections at their jobs—the lucky ones did, anyway.

My extroverted friends who drank had favorite pubs where they gathered but that wasn't me either.

I was still floundering. But I knew what I wanted.

I wanted to get to know my neighbors and my neighborhood better. And I wanted to keep writing.

# Hint 4: Feel your a-ha! moment in your bones.

In January 2012, I was in San Francisco interviewing people for a book I'd begun writing with my friend Bas. David (who I've since come to consider a friend) asked me to meet him at the coworking space where he often worked. The interview was fun—David's story of leaping away from financially-lucrative-but-energy-draining work was eerily similar to my own story. The coworking space there was bigger than any in Seattle at the time. Its bones were utterly delightful—huge, open, beautiful—and the space buzzed with vibrant, we're-changing-the-world energy.

Living in Seattle's Central District for 10 years had changed me. I'd learned to care deeply about neighborhood representation in the spaces I occupy. And it hit me immediately: almost everyone in the space was young and white. There were a few women present but mostly it was men. The space looked different but the people looked eerily similar to those in most high-tech companies up and down the coast. This was not at all what the walk through the diverse neighborhood to get to the space had primed me to expect. During the delightful interview with utterly delightful David, my mind kept pushing up these thoughts: "Where are all the black people, older people, and women? How can coworking as a movement legitimately claim to be a major improvement on the old ways of working if we don't address these neighborhood representation issues?" We. I was saying we. More foreshadowing. Before I even knew it, I was already a coworking space creator. Already a neighborhood mover and shaker (which I prefer to activist—I'm not a fan of –ists as ends in my own labels, that's just me). I walked down the street away from that space thinking "I could do coworking better than that. We could do coworking better than that in the CD."

That's where the idea to turn our home into a coworking space was born: at a collision within me. A collision between my own longing to connect with my neighbors and community (and my many not-long-lasting-enough attempts to do so on my own), my own desire to give back to my amazing neighborhood, and my own gut-deep certainty that I could do something better than how I'd just seen it done, even though they appeared to have far more money and resources and energy and space and really cool natural-wood tables than me. I didn't know how I would do better. I just knew that I could. That we could. For a brief moment, I knew. Down into my bones.

Within days the idea to turn our home into a coworking space just appeared. It showed up as a "Duh. Of course I will be doing this." thought. I was a little nervous, but mostly I just wanted to get on with it now that I had an idea I knew deep down would work and that I myself would stick with long enough to make a difference at.

Story wrangler tip: "I just knew. I didn't know how I would do it. I just knew that I could." are words I've heard again and again as a researcher, community story wrangler, and community member. When these words are spoken, stop what you are doing, focus, and listen closely. Record in some way. You will use what you learn at some point in time, likely again and again and again.

## Hint 5: Watch your energy skyrocket at the idea.

I was so excited by the idea of turning our home into a coworking space when it finally dawned on me that I immediately shared the idea with several close friends and invited them to work at the space. Even before I remembered that I should've asked my spouse and housemates if they'd be ok with it first. Whoops.

Always a fun conversation.

"Honey, how would you feel about having our home become a free coworking space and, yeah, I already sort of invited my friends from the Seattle Consultants Grotto group to come here on Wednesdays?" Fortunately, we had an ACOF (always count of forgiveness) kind of partnership.

I've since learned that a lot of people who show up to work in an in-home space show up already in love with the idea. They show up ready to make it work together. I've learned that in-home coworking spaces can become beacons, magnets, wide-range receivers, and markets for others interested in having more ACOF relationships in their lives. But I'm getting ahead of myself.

For me, this is the most important hint here in the Imagining the Space section. Because as I've learned to pay close attention to and honor my own energy in the coworking space, I've also learned to notice—and point out—the same energy spikes in others. They're often tough to see for ourselves. I've also learned how to honor declining energy and how to let go of things at the appropriate time as energy lags. Being able to trust my own energy—far ahead of having reasons and answers—makes me a lot more fun to be around in general and a far more efficient and decisive decision maker than I used to be. On the down side, I'm more to deal with as a spouse now. Daniel gets to figure out what to do with Lori statements such as: "We need to move to an island. I don't know why. I'm sure we'll figure it out when we get there."

# Hint 6: Imagine just three people in the space as enough.

Part of the reason I could imagine our in-home coworking space working was that I knew my friends Tim and Diane would come work with me some Wednesdays in the beginning. They were both in the position to come work with me often back then. Most of my friends and neighbors weren't due to day-jobs and distance. Even if nobody else ever came to the coworking space, having these two friends come work with me once in a while, I decided, was enough for me. Just getting to see them more regularly would be a win. And it was.

I learned that having two deeply trusted friends willing to show up with me in the space is more than enough. At the beginning, they got me through the important humility-generating "We Built It. We're Here! Why Isn't Anyone Else Showing Up?" stage of creating a coworking space in your home.

Diane is so warm and open and smart. Plus she's an amazing baker. People who bake and/or cook are invaluable in-home coworking space members. Word of her amazing cookies spread, drawing more coworkers some weeks than anything I ever tried. Of course, I once over-indulged in her chocolate chip oatmeal espresso cookies and couldn't fall asleep until after 4 a.m., but that's really my failing, not hers.

Tim was the most generous-with-his-time person I knew. That's still true. He's a fellow nomad. Likes to wander around and sample and think about and share many connections and ideas and things, like I do. Tim and I still regularly co-work together (as regularly as two work nomads do anything). One of the joys of an in-home coworking space is that people like Tim and I—people who mentally, spiritually, and/or physically move around a lot, like hummingbirds—are welcome to be as present, or non-present, as we'd like. The only strings attached in our space are those fine, invisible and stretchy webs that we weave for ourselves.

Today I can see that periodically popping back into this "Why isn't anyone here today?" stage—as an in-home coworking space—is both inevitable and fabulous. Humility is a good thing. At least for us. It means that the community you do end up with is fan-frickin-tastic and real. Like ice cream, community is both harder to make and at least 100 times better if you make it yourself. The people who walk in and quickly leave because only one or two other humans, and a cat, are in the space at the moment, are those leading with "What can these people give me?" Those who show up and talk until they imagine themselves as a vital community member—because there aren't dozens present—are rock-star awesome. Only rock-star awesome community members return to our little space. It's like magic.

## Hint 7: Receive input and support from those you share the home with.

I spent a week or two tossing ideas around with spouse Daniel before I started hosting coworking. I was so excited about the idea that I immediately wanted to do a million different things. We could turn the entire little cottage behind our house into a coworking space! We could be open 7 days/week! We could use the space for classes, discussions, and workshops! Or I could even evolve the space into a more independent space at a more neighborhood-centric location. Waaah! Cowork all the things!

Most of Daniel's task involved reflecting my energy back to me so I could see it. And reeling in my excitement and energy a tiny bit to help me focus on what mattered most. We landed on experimenting with coworking out of the main house 1 day/week, for 8 hours, to see if we even liked doing it. I am so glad we did, because while I didn't see it at the time, one day/week honored my own move-around-a lot, hummingbird nature. Had I started with 5 or even 3 days/week, I suspect I'd have quit within a few months.

I then took the idea to housemates Chris and Emil, and backyard cottage-renter Kristine, asking if they'd support the 1 day/week coworking in-the-main-house idea and asking if they had any concerns. I received only support and positive responses. Good sign. I felt I didn't need to ask dogs and cats, because I knew their loving presence would hold steady no matter what we did.

I expected the folks I lived with to want to have deeper conversations about the idea. But everybody else was so busy with their own lives that what I received was 3- to 5-word responses in passing or via text or email. All variations on "Good idea" and "Great! Go for it!" and "Good luck with that!" and "I'll attend when I can!" Nobody else in my house-hold seemed to think it was a particularly life-changing idea or event. But it would be life changing for me. And that was enough. Based on past experience, I knew the guys would eventually figure out that it was a really good idea. ;-)

# Hint 8: Receive input and support from neighbors.

Once all my in-house people said good idea/yes, I then talked to the neighbors that I knew up and down our block to see what they thought about the idea.

Fortunately, thanks to 10 years of shared dinners, tool sharing, annual block parties, front-porch gatherings, and the community pit-stop Central Cinema (half a block from us—yay Kate and Kevin!), I already knew roughly 30 of my neighbors. The Central District is cool that way. We even already had an informal neighbor email list that I could use.

I contacted all neighbors I thought might have concerns about the idea, and I asked them if they had any concerns. I expected someone to worry about impact to street parking in our busy, center-of-city neighborhood, and I created a detailed approach to ensuring this wouldn't be an issue before I sent the message. I woefully underestimated my neighbors (as I tended to do back then). Here's a sampling of what I heard back:

"Lori, I LOVE this idea. We're actually renting out desks at my employer's office downtown… It's been great to get to know new people, have people to bounce ideas off of, and made for some really interesting lunch conversations….I'd love to be my own 'boss' and just write….I may take you up on the offer. This is very, very cool. I hope you get quite a collective together! Thanks for doing this."

and

"That sounds so great! I wish I was in a better position to jump in with freelancing. What a great adventure. I hope it works out! Keep me posted!"

and

"Hi Lori. This is such a cool idea! Unfortunately, I have to be at my desk at work five days a week. Boo."

and

"Great idea! I'll pass this on to friends who may be interested."


Not a single fear about impact to street parking! Or fear about the space at all. Why had I worried so much?

I didn't talk to all neighbors. In a dense urban neighborhood like ours, that'd be impossible for one person: where did our neighbors even end? But I spoke to enough on our one block that I felt more certain that the idea would be accepted by others. And the fact that we were experimenting with the idea—just trying it out for one 8-hour day/week when most of them were away at work—helped me believe that we wouldn't unduly inconvenience neighbors in our efforts to find and build community for ourselves.

## Hint 9: Imagine the space as a gift by neighbors for neighbors.

The week I told our neighbors that I'd like to turn our house into a free community coworking space one day/week was a pretty cool week. The wave of support they sent my way actually made me cry.

Wow. We'd lived in our neighborhood 10 years at that point. Most of those years I'd been so busy with my day job plus going to school full time that I hadn't had enough time/energy to connect with neighbors deeply.

It dawned on me as I heard back from my remarkably supportive neighbors that this wasn't actually my idea at all. This was a need my neighborhood had surfaced in me, directly connected to others' needs in the neighborhood.

I shifted from thinking "I suck. I can't do anything right. What should I do?" to "I'm a genius for coming up with this idea!" to "I am so very lucky to live here." That last one feels the best.

I thought to myself "I'm so lucky to live where I live, surrounded by these neighbors. I can't wait to meet more of them!"

That's the energy I brought with me to the space as I unlocked our door for the first time: the energy of gratitude and thankfulness for what we already had. The belief that neighbors are a gift. A desire to give back to a neighborhood that had given us so much.

The space itself started as a gift. And it's been a gift almost every day since—whether I'm there or not.

Every human, dog, and cat that has walked through the door since has been a gift: most in the moment, a few in hindsight.

# Hint 10: Accept help with imagination from kind strangers.

Before I worked in Unlocked-Front Door land, I was really scared at first. Terrified. What if a total asshole walked in? Or a criminal? What if an accident happened and we got sued? Or, God forbid, what if a whole gang of extroverts wandered in? Yikes.

Instead of focusing on that fear and planning around it, imagine facing your fears with one friend, then two. Then with small waves of new friends and neighbors who regularly show up. Imagine learning to live with your fears together—across a whole neighborhood. That's what happened to me. Or imagine that somewhere in the process of living with your fears together one day you—and all the people you adore who regularly show up in the space—become total bad ass kind ninja humans together. People who:

- look out for each other and keep each other safe and the whole neighborhood safer
- show up bearing ideas and energy and food and drinks and work and play and skills and tips and tools all as gifts for each other
- find more playfulness and honesty and friendship within themselves and within increasing circles of others
- reveal to themselves how amazing they and their neighbors and neighborhood actually are, and from that place of deep respect and wonder, play with improvement together and with other neighbors doing the same
- learn to play with ideas and projects and with complete strangers and people they couldn't imagine playing with before (for me, that'd be government officials—playful government officials exist, who knew?!)
- share, swap, barter, re-use, gift, and pay each other, revealing hidden abundance
- leave lasting legacies for current and future neighbors/friends/residents/citizens
- know that they have it within themselves to effect lasting change for themselves, instead of waiting for someone else to do it
- reimagine the community space as being inside themselves—transportable everywhere they go

Three years ago, I just didn't want to be lonely working at home by myself anymore. What I ended up with was all this.

This is my world now. It's an honor, a deep privilege, just to be here. Just to be in their presence. I know that now. I live that now. Almost every day. Almost everywhere I go.

# Hint 11: Don't imagine the space.

Create a community space in your home and see what happens for yourself. For something both simple and deeply important, like this, I've learned that it's better just to dream together as you go.

Running the Space

Hint 12: Show up, unlock the door, take out the trash, and clean the bathroom.

Running an in-home community space isn't a glamour gig and it isn't for people who don't like to get their hands dirty. At least 90% of running the space is reliably showing up, unlocking the door, taking out the trash, wiping down the counters, sweeping/vacuuming, washing hand and kitchen towels, and cleaning the bathroom.

Do this every week for a year and you, too, will be called a Leader in the Free Coworking Movement. If not by online magazine Sharable, than by me. We're all leaders here.

All the rest of the hints in this section—and everything else you choose to do when you run your own space—are icing on the cake. Entirely up to you. Entirely changeable by you. These hints are for those coming next certain to do this even better than I did it. People like Nicole, Forrest, Elyse, Jane, and Natja.

# Hint 13: Don't run the space.

Working in the space is the fun part anyway. To the best of my ability, back when I ran the space I sought to honor all community members, including myself, as a community member first, above the role of "official person running the space" or any other role needed. If this matters to you, do it, don't just talk about how much it matters to you.

Work in the space. Collaborate with others. Do your own work. Talk about your failures and your successes. Ask for advice. Ask for help. Share things. Tell people to make themselves at home and go digging through the cupboards until they find what they need. Teach a few people where everything is and ask them to teach others. Bake cookies. Play with the dog in the back yard. Learn to make things and fix things. Make tea. Tell jokes. Ask others to be admins of the Facebook page (or whatever) for the space. Demonstrate all the things it's ok to do in the space by doing them yourself when possible.

As you get comfortable with the community, one of the best things you can do to run a space like this is to leave. Leave for an hour, then 3 hours, then a day, or a month, or a season. Ask others to run the space in your absence. This is likely a bias of mine. All my favorite community and coworking spaces are those in which the people running the space are indistinguishable from the people working in the space and lots of different faces are seen running things. No need to go crazy like I did and eventually move away and have somebody else show up to live in the house and offer to take over running the space entirely. (But that's really fun too.)

Yes, there will be people who want someone official running things, although fewer than you might expect. It's not a bad thing to occasionally be that for someone, to ease them into working in this very different world than they're used working in. But I tried not to make a habit of it back when I ran things, and Nicole's even better at this than me. I try to be honest about what I want and don't want and then live that. In my case, I want a community in which everyone who considers themselves a member is comfortable running the space or is at least willing to do so when they want to be there but Nicole or I can't be. And I want a community in which everyone who considers themselves a visitor is welcomed and treated with generosity and kindness to the point that they're likely to come back or tell their friends even if they themselves don't want to be here.

The space teaches us—we're all students within it. If you're a control freak, expect to learn a cubic ton of approaches for just letting go. If you're super easy-going, expect to learn a similar ton of approaches for getting things done and making things happen. If you're talkative, expect to learn to honor silence. If you're silent, expect to learn to honor happy chatter. If you have to take a phone call, expect to receive a collective death-glare until you learn to take phone conversations into an empty room or outside.

## Hint 14: Connect with other people learning in the same direction online.

A few months before I got the idea to turn our home into a coworking space, a person I didn't know (a fan of my Collective Self blog at the time) added me to a Facebook group called Coworking Worldwide. I didn't realize I was even part of this community until he added me to it. He saw something in me that I didn't see in myself yet—all the way from Europe. So cool. I now consider him a friend. Thanks Bert-Ola!

I'd been lurking in that Facebook group for months, watching what others in the coworking community were doing, not realizing that the idea to morph our home into a coworking space would come to me. I respected and trusted many people in this online community immediately and to this today. The month I started our coworking space, I found multiple favorite resources:

- The Coworking Seattle group (now, the Seattle Collaborative Space Alliance)
- Coworking News and their Global Coworking calendar
- Desk Wanted
- Global Coworking Unconference Conference

I began talking to the people behind these groups and sharing stories and ideas, even recipes.

The specific resources and people I found aren't important, except to me. Find your own resources.

The point is to find just a handful of key resources and people to learn with online following your own energy at the beginning—not hundreds before you start. Diversity across key resources is a fantastic goal. And more isn't necessarily better at first. It's easy to spin within research mode forever these days. Pick a few resources and people and get to know them well enough that you'd share a personal story or family recipe with them. Make friends. Three friends online—running spaces in other places—are more valuable than 3 million online resources.

# Hint 15: Connect with other people learning in the same direction locally.

Within a week or so of opening our in-home coworking space, I contacted people at the two more formal coworking spaces I knew about in neighboring neighborhoods in Seattle at the time: Office Nomads on Capitol Hill and The Hub in Pioneer Square.

I told them I loved what they're doing for our community. I told them that if they learned of anyone in our neighborhoods who couldn't afford their spaces or liked the idea of coworking but didn't quite mesh with their larger spaces, that I'd appreciate it if they'd tell them about us on Wednesdays. And I'd send people their way too. Again, I received a ton of support.

From Office Nomads: "Hi Lori! Wow – what an amazing email that was to get! I am so excited that you'll be hosting regular Jellies at your place – that's fantastic! We'll be sure to share the info. And I'll have to swing by sometime – that's just a block away from the last house I lived in, and just a few blocks away from my new place (I'm also in the CD). Let me know if there is anything that you need, or if you need help getting the word out. Take good care and thanks again for all the kind words." - Susan

From The Hub: "Hi Lori, This is wonderful news! I'd be happy to spread the word to our fellow Hub members, including in our next member email. I used to live in the CD and would have loved this option had I the chance – so am excited to pass the word on to others, too! Thanks so much for sharing" - Lindsey

At the time (three years ago now), in my blog I wrote "I haven't met these folks face to face yet, but I already think they rock and am planning to become friends with Susan at Office Nomads and Lindsey at the Hub whether they like it or not!"

I'm still friends with many people in the Seattle Collaborative Space Alliance—people who taught me that we have no competitors in Seattle—even though a few of us have moved on to other things. These people taught me the value of seeing our little space as part of a vast network of spaces—any one of which we could connect with, share about/with, and point people to who needed something beyond what our space can offer. We still give out Space Traveler mugs to people who work in 5 or more SCSA spaces. Tim's at 4. Geez, Tim, get the lead out!

Friends learning in the same direction locally support the expansion of your imagination in a grounded way. Staying grounded in the real world—which a coworking space can do for often-online people like me—will move you into action faster, even if it's just to make cookies. I would again argue that less is more in this early stage. Make one or two friends. You can't see the future yet. As your energy shifts, so will the resources and people you're learning with. The kind of diversity you as an individual need most will come through the coworking space itself—much faster than trying to find it on your own up front, in my experience. New friends, and even strangers, will push things to you in a coworking space, instead of you constantly trying to wade through the knowledge of the world, trying to find what you need. Google may feel like a friend, but Google is no Susan. Susan sends me actual people and specific ideas and resources and food and dog stories and me-appropriate humor and empathy—sometimes before I myself know I need them. She magically appeared in our space the other day after I proclaimed loudly/threatened online that I was writing this flash nonfiction book in just one month and really needed help, fast. Suck it Google. Susan is pure magic.

## Hint 16: Imagine the whole space as one big experiment and small pilot ideas.

In the beginning, I strongly suspected that we would love having our home be a free coworking space. At the time, in fact, Daniel and I imagined converting our back rental cottage into a larger community space. I even began imagining one day opening a more formal space.

But we didn't know for sure that we would love it. Or what the future held. What if we hated it? What if we were called elsewhere?

So we decided to start small: one day a week, for eight hours. It seemed like a good way to test the idea. And we figured "If the community here grows, then we will too." We've been small piloting ideas ever since.

Small piloting ideas visibly appears to create lots of small piloting of ideas. And lots of demonstrations that it's ok to try, make mistakes, tweak things, and try again. Doesn't make you a loser. It makes you awesome.

This whole damn life of ours is one big experiment. Why do we pretend otherwise? Why do we take ourselves so seriously that we end up freaking out and hurting ourselves and each other in the process? Some days in the coworking space work beyond my wildest dreams. Some days don't.

Some days you might be sitting there coworking with a cat and nobody else. "More chairs for me!" thinks the cat.

All days are a gift—some in the moment and others in hindsight.

Especially if you struggle with risk taking and with regularly failing, like I do, or aren't allowed to or can't experiment and play elsewhere, in-home coworking spaces are fantastic places to be.

Every day is an experiment for everyone who shows up. You're all in the same boat. The S.S. What Could We Try Next?

## Hint 17: Play.

For me, play started even before the space opened. I played with thinking about what I like to do and don't like to do and I decided to make these both ok and visible from the beginning. For example, although I would be the one unlocking and opening the door each week, and telling people about the space at first, I didn't want to be in charge of our coworking space. What I really liked doing was gathering, hearing, documenting, and telling community stories. I wanted to do that and be a member of the space, not a person in charge. I like to work in groups only where everyone is a leader (or nobody is, depending on how people in the group feel about the word leader). However, some people like visible leaders, so I played with having those too.

Grady dog and cats Batman, Bella, and Joe were already a group that was really good at making the space playful and fun. So, I made them the executive staff to formally run our space. Their original titles, based on what they loved doing most:

- Grady, Exercise and Outdoor Activities Director
- Joe, Director of Napping
- Batman, Chief Play and Innovation Officer
- Bella, Dispute Creation and Resolution Smackdown Specialist (responsible for starting and breaking up fights for the pure fun of it)

Grady later also became the Director of Marketing after he got lost for 4 hours, the whole neighborhood rallied to help find him, and 10 new people showed up in the space the following week as a result. This was 8 more new people than I'd ever managed to bring into the space in a week.

In the early days, if people had questions that would be better answered by our executive staff, I would direct them to the appropriate cat or dog. Grady would encourage people outside to take walks with him and encourage people to throw tennis balls in the back yard. Batman would demand people play laser chase with him or at least allow him to play inside their open backpacks and bags. Or he'd sit in his own chair at the table and stare at us until we laughed. Joe would sleep on people who worked in the living room, and chew on Tim's wool socks. Bella would walk by and lovingly, or not, swat the other cats in the head. As a leadership team, they were flaw-filled and flawless. They created just one rule for the space: People with severe dog or cat allergies have to sit outside or work elsewhere.

It's your home, your space. Imagine what makes you happy. Do what makes you happy. If you want to make an emergency neighborhood party-preparedness kit one afternoon together, instead of your individual work efforts, for example, do it! Playfulness helps you make space within yourself for others to be themselves and do the same, and it draws playful others to you—complimentary and amazing others—far beyond what you can imagine. I can imagine quite a bit now. And I'm still surprised by the awesomeness that walks in through that open front door.

## Hint 18: Reimagine yourself as often as you'd like.

When we were kids, we reimagined ourselves all the time. What were you? A teacher? A parent? A puppy? A monkey? A tree? A chef? A famous sports hero? A fireman? A doctor? A racecar driver? A character out of a favorite book? A squirrel? A horse? An airplane? The captain of a boat in hot lava or surrounded by sharks? A detective? A super-hero? A dolphin? A cloud? A builder of great buildings? The fluffy part of the dandelion flower that blows away in the wind? All of the above?

If it is nothing else, a coworking space is a place for adults to keep reimagining themselves. For those of us who stick with these spaces, they can be places where we are reminded that we are better at self-reimagination now—not worse—than when we were kids. How many adults believe that they are less creative and imaginative now than when they were kids? Not me. Not anymore. In the years I've been connected to our space my titles, online signatures, and/or business card titles have shifted regularly:

- Self-Organizing Groups Researcher (2011)
- Community Story Wrangler (early 2012)
- Coworking Space Holder (early 2012)
- Network Weaver (mid 2012)
- Open Scholar (early 2013)
- Hopscotch CD Event Co-imaginer (mid 3013)
- Community Member (mid 2013)
- Home Canning Guru (mid 2013)
- Community Gardener (mid 2013)
- Writer (mid 2013)
- Pirate (late 2013)
- Neighbor (late 2013)
- Dog Mom (late 2013)
- Poet (mid 2014)
- Mermaid (late 2014)
- Improv Troupe Team Member (late 2014)
- Family Elder (late 2014)
- Dragon (early 2015)
- Care Partner (early 2015)
- Flash Non-Fiction Author (early 2015)
- Space Runner (early 2015)

The reality is that I'm all these things. The space gave me the courage to fully see that, name that, and own what I am. No need to be strange like me. Be strange like you. My point is that I own my own titles. I play with what I am now. The space taught me to be proud of what I am both in person and on paper. I've had this title-shifting ability my whole life—even during my 20 years as a corporate employee—but I didn't fully share it, or recognize it as a gift, until I became a member in our space.

You might be tempted to make your space all about community changing or world changing. That's fantastic. And. It starts with you. If you notice and honor and talk about and make visible the changes in yourself regularly—creating wordless space and open invitation for others to do the same—you might be shocked one day to find that that was more than enough to bring forth change within you, your community, and our world.

## Hint 19: Reimagine relationship building and spreading the word.

From my perspective, like all other visible roles in the space, relationship building and spreading the word (what some people unfortunately call "marketing"—bleh) is best done by everyone. I'm lucky. Based on past experience, I came into running our space knowing that I am definitely not better at relationship building or spreading the word than anyone else. What I am better at is living and telling my own story. Like everyone is in my world.

For me, spreading word about the space is about making it easier for other community members to recognize themselves as both vital community members (for example, by putting their pictures on the walls, supporting what they're doing, connecting them to potentially important-for-them others, sharing their events and work, etc.) and vital storytellers (for example, by listening to their stories, asking them to tell their stories, thanking them for sharing ours). And it's about sharing community stories. These aren't my tasks because I run the space, which I haven't for more than a year now. These are the tasks I love to do. Yours may be similar or wildly different.

Our most successful "marketing campaigns" to date:

- The day Grady dog got lost during rush hour by following a stranger (who dressed like Chris) home, and the neighborhood—in person and online—came out in full force to help us for several hours. And how we ended up weeping and hugging a total stranger in a narrow alley after dark in our "dangerous" neighborhood. Grady, who'd been fed dinner and then watched a movie with his new dog and human friends, didn't understand what all the fuss was about. But so many people showed up in the space the next week that his title changed to Director of Marketing.

- The time Chris, Lori, and mama squirrel spent a day rescuing four baby squirrels trapped in our attic and I learned that both mama squirrels, and people named Chris, are excellent team players and total bad asses. I learned that I am too, not despite my tears and fears, but because of them.

- The time—before they'd even met in person—that Knox of Jackson Commons and Lori decided to work together to create Hopscotch CD—1.8 Miles of Fun!, a then-new annual neighborhood event centered around two miles of temporary hopscotch path, fun, and people doing whatever the frick they want to do to celebrate the neighborhood. From full-scale carnivals to magic and glitter booths to yard sales to chalk art to little free libraries being built to libraries on wheels to free books for kids to neighborhood history walks, edible weed learning walks, women's friendship walks, Guinness Record book attempts, and free music/jam sessions/musical instruments, the CD is FUCKING AWESOME! (forgive me the all caps, it had to be said)

- That August when we hosted a Seattle Collaborative Space Alliance BBQ to celebrate ourselves as collaborative spaces on International Coworking Day. Visitors stopped and dropped off sushi for 50 people! And most people brought enough food or drinks for everyone, so we ended up giving food and drinks away for weeks! Realizing that it's ok to have little money and no plan as long as you have friends to imagine great things with and neighbors to eat with.

- That time Fisher and Sean turned our buckets of excess strawberries and rhubarb into popsicles and gave them away to surprised and delighted people in parks via bicycles and their pop-up Popcycles idea. Love those guys. The impact these two have gone on to make in the Seattle community today is stunning. I'm so proud of them. I had no doubt.

- That time 3-blocks-away neighbor Tabitha made postcards, and later buttons, for the space out of the kindness of her heart, finally giving me the courage to trust in the kindness of my neighbors and strangers and spread them around neighborhood coffee shops and businesses. Locally made and shared fliers and buttons are cool.

- Telling the story of the big, round, 10-person 500-year table that our friends created for the space out of the old fir/gym floor from Garfield High School's remodeling project. God I love that table and working and eating at that table and talking about that table. Telling people it was built to last (can be sanded new every 10 years for 500 years) by craftsmen in South Park (wood top) and Georgetown (metal base) out of Central District reclaimed wood. I'm going to be telling its story the rest of my days. If I ever get my hands on a time machine, I'm going to stalk that table across all 500 of its years.

- Every time a community member plans and hosts an after-hours event in the space, amazing things happen. Too. Much. To. Say. See Hint 20.

- The day I sat wondering what to do about the coworking space because I wanted to move to Whidbey Island, and after 20 years in the city, have a wide-open horizon again like I did as a kid, and then Nicole—a stranger to me—walked in the door, sat down, and said "There is asbestos in our apartment's ductwork. We have to move. Do you know any good places to live around here?" And I said "How about here?" And she said "Could we still run the coworking space?" and I said "Oh my God, Hell yes!!!!!"

- The day Nicole announced on Facebook that she couldn't host coworking anymore because of her new daytime-hours day job and 5 people cyber-yelled almost simultaneously "I'll do it! I'll help!"

These aren't marketing campaigns. They're just our stories. They involve real people slowing down together, growing closer as people, helping each other out, being touched by the experience, and sharing their story/our story with others. In our world, everyone who touches us becomes both a character in our story and a storyteller of that story in their own way. The task of marketing as a specialty isn't needed, because everybody who wants to share our stories does it fluidly and naturally in their own way, to their own people, and everybody who doesn't doesn't.

## Hint 20: Say "Yes!" to people who want to host after-hours events in the space.

Anytime a community member plans and hosts an after-hours event in the space, amazing things happen. Those who were there will know:

- Christopher's honey tasting party (people who taste 90 different honeys talk really fast)
- Narisa's beer tasting party (we're exactly like the United Nations, only with beer)
- Jane and Narisa's dumpling creation extravaganza (yes, there actually is such a thing as too many dumplings—that would be 500+ dumplings for 9 people)
- Tabitha's Saturday crafternoon series involved making things such as monsters, sock monkeys, guerilla gardening seed balls, garden markers and painted rocks (making all the things is fun, especially when someone who knows what's she's doing helps us)
- Kristine's Stich N' Bitch session (more bitching than stitching, as I recall)
- Fisher's monthly group facilitator's meetings (wicked smart people who brought amazing food, used really cool big words, and left the kitchen ten times cleaner than they found it)
- Knox and I hosting Hopscotch CD planning/creating/doing meetings, and associated template-creation and rock-painting gatherings with Kenton, Tabitha, Derryl and Sharon, Jane and Ryan, Scotia, Meegan, and others. (beyond fun to be working at home, especially for me: the introvert semi-traumatized by all the large groups I had to go talk to)
- Angela—impromptu CD carnival planner extraordinaire—bringing her meetings to our house to make cross-event-coordination easier. (Young people rock)
- Seattle Department of Neighborhoods people coming to our house to help us coordinate ourselves and our grant paperwork for Hopscotch CD. (OMFG. They came to us. City officials came to our house for a meeting. We're so blessed. Amazing.)
- Mumi Tuesdays (one year, Eva the puppy invited Mumi the puppy to do dog coworking every Tuesday, to wear each other out, and keep Lori and Sayumi from exhausting themselves trying to wear out their puppies separately)
- Game nights hosted by all sorts of people (because games are almost always fun, the exception being that one 4-hour-long overly dark and complicated one that Narisa described as "less fun than death")
- Daniel hosting his company's director-level offsite retreats in the space (office-building folks learn that working from home together fosters creativity and comradery, plus hey, that's 10 fewer rich white people certain that the CD is dangerous) ;-)
- Thanksgiving dinners (so much family, so much food)
- Sci Fi Fridays (a long tradition in a house oddly full of lovers of the weird, the quirky, and the Sci Fi. Live long and prosper. Rest in peace, Leonard Nemoy.)
- Neighborhood parents gathering in the space to organize and resist a school district's short-sighted decision (I have no idea what you're talking about, but go, activist parents/neighbors, go! Better schools help us all.)

- Nicole's couch-based-film-festival hosting (damn, wish I'd been there—the pictures were great)

- Isaac hosting stand-up-comedian writing sessions (I suspect these might be some of my favorite humans ever. I wish I wasn't too awkwardly shy to speak to them. People with the courage to speak in public scare me.)

- Elyse hosting salons about the impacts of gentrification (Is anyone else noticing how utterly amazing young people now are? I'm constantly blown away.)

## Hint 21: Become friends with people in other coworking and collaborative spaces in your area.

For example, people in... Other coworking spaces. And artist spaces. And maker spaces of any kind. Places where people work together and share the cost of the space itself, if not the ownership. Intentional co-ops and collaboration spaces. Community gardens. Community centers run by the city and neighborhood people together. Community-focused small barbershops and hair salons, coffee shops, bars, newspapers, and grocery stores. Anarchist collectives. Homeless shelters. Backyard barter events. Whole-block yard salers. Anywhere where everyone gets some say in how their collective works.

Seattle has Tent Cities for homeless people that move around every month or two—onto the land of churches, schools, and other available excess land. A perfect solution? I can't say, I'm not a core community member. Yet I've spent enough time with residents to see that they are run by residents themselves and better run than the corporations I've worked for. Beyond what they do for themselves, they pick up trash, and monitor security, for at least two blocks in every direction around themselves: together. Don't judge collective books by their covers. The smaller they are the more visible their hearts and their inner workings as organizations can often be.

This was crucial for me running the space. These are the people I asked important questions of, like:

- Nobody is here again today. What are we doing wrong?
- Where do I get high-quality tables and chairs? Ok, what about when I have no money?
- We want to do _____. Have you tried this? What happened?
- Can I come and work in your space today? I can't get any work done in mine this week.
- What could we do together to make our lives more fun and our stories even more interesting? To entice more people out of working in their individual homes, or outside of their day job spaces, and come to work in all our spaces?

This is also important for your members and your visitors. The more your community members visit other spaces, the more intertwined and interesting (and I'd argue, better) your lives become.

Not all visitors to your space are best served by your space. For example, when I ran our space, we didn't want people with cat or dog allergies, because we couldn't make the space pet-hair free. Hell, I couldn't even keep Batman off people's laps. And I didn't want little kids in the space during work hours because the house wasn't kid proof and the space was small enough that there was nowhere to send kids to play. I kept a growing list of nearby alternative working spaces for people with pet allergies and people who wanted to work with their kids. I also connected the kid folks with friends of mine who were working on creating a coworking space with a daycare center in it. And I encouraged people to turn their own homes into coworking spaces. Because awesome! How awesome would that be?

Office Nomads—7 years old now and a grandparent space to so many others—is in Capitol Hill, an adjacent neighborhood to the Central District. In the three years since I first spoke to Susan, I've spent a lot of time there. They introduced me to people running spaces all over the city. They told me uplifting stories when I was sad that nobody was showing up in our space. Later I became a member there for a year to support them when they expanded and doubled the size of their space (not that I ever got much better at talking to people beyond those running the place--Susan, Jacob, Chelsea, and Alex back then, plus all the dogs).

We've created cross-Seattle-Collaborative-Space-Alliance promotion ideas together, interviewed each other, loaned equipment to each other, made useful gifts for each other (like books and a video showing a day in the life of a space). Susan and I support each other to this day. We still share people with each other and share each other's stories. I credit Office Nomads with the fact that Collective Self is still in operation today. Because Alex (who used to work at Office Nomads) and her fiancé Nicole now live in our home, and Nicole continued running Collective Self coworking when I left. Now Elyse, who also lives in the home and was shared by Susan with us, is planning to help with coworking too. We literally couldn't have done it without them.

The people of Office Nomads are more than just life-long friends to me and to Collective Self Coworking. They are living examples that community members are deep gifts: valuable beyond all understanding and all measure. This isn't just something we believe. It is something that we experience and see all the time, thanks to them/us: the people who just keep showing up for each other.

Hint 22: Deep welcome doesn't begin at your door, it begins on the sidewalk and in the street.

I began noticing who we naturally draw to us and that who we draw shifts as we shift. We've naturally drawn lots of work nomads. We've drawn introverts and flexible and patient extroverts. We naturally draw other lonely neighbors, neighbors interested in lasting community connections but not finding them in traditional work or community spaces, people interested in neighborhood history, in giving back to the neighborhood they live in, artists, gardeners, illustrators, graphic designers, programmers, game designers, event planners, academics, food lovers, teachers, stand-up comedians, great cooks and bakers, gracious hosts, people who love to experiment, and people who love playing games. We naturally draw white women and men, gay women and men, Asian women and men, and travelers from other countries and states (reflections of who lives in the house). People ages 20 to 50.

Deep welcome is something else. Deep welcome is stepping outside, and offering your hand to connect with those who aren't naturally drawn to you. Our coworking space is helping us make this happen. Even for a quiet, scared, introvert writer like me eventually it wasn't enough to be open, free, and happily working with a small group of others inside our space. Eventually we found ourselves spilling outside to work hand-in-hand with our neighbors on deeply fun and deeply meaningful neighborhood beautification and neighborhood pain-reducing projects. Because we'd seen first-hand that our neighbors are so very worth the effort. We wanted more.

This isn't easy. But it can be simple. We started by involving ourselves in simple neighbor-led events (like Hopscotch CD, and the carnival and Guinness Record attempts that arose around it), art making for the neighborhood (mini-library creation, garden art making, guerilla gardening seed balls), and small gardening projects (turning our parking strip into a neighbor garden and supporting a couple of other neighbors interested in doing the same). This expanded our draw. Black neighbors walked in our doors. Many neighborhood- and city-level dreamers, event planners, artists and activists come now too. Once you visit the deep welcome space, I think you're changed for good. I won't settle for less than deep welcome now. I'm happy and honored to come to you if you don't want to/ can't come to me.

The people coworking and connected to the space today astonish me. They're imagining far larger gardening projects, such as turning parking strips into neighbor gardens up and down 21st street. Members and friends of the space today are actively tackling neighborhood- and city-wide issues by, for example, speaking out against a new youth jail being built, teaching more complete versions of neighborhood and city history, bringing bike-sharing to the city, supporting people with dementia and their care partners across the city, working for safer streets for people walking and biking in the neighborhood, protesting unsafe work and transportation practices, improving air quality, marching in protests to show solidarity with neighbors, creating leadership institutes for people of color, hosting salons about the impacts of gentrification, using art to teach life skills, teaching colleagues about options for freelance worker healthcare, hosting film festivals, becoming poets, running collaborative spaces themselves, and hosting neighborhood-centered comedy shows. And that's just off the top of my head.

Most strangers I meet now tend to astonish me with their awesomeness too. Mostly because I listen a lot longer than I used to. I know I can come across to some as naïve and optimistic about the world. But that feels like a remarkably small down side to living your life in awe of the people around you.

## Hint 23: Embrace both welcome and unwelcome as part of your routine now.

I need both to grow. This space gives me plenty of both. Some people show up adoring me and/or the space already. Nothing I could do or say would change their minds. They love me. Just as I am. This feels great. I learned to let this feel great. Most people show up open to the idea of experimenting with coworking. They get that what we're doing is creating community together, in the moment, and that one day will look completely different from the next. These are the people I have fun with. I learned to let it be fun when it was fun. With these folks I feel welcome. A few people show up scared to talk to others or just busy or simply uninterested in talking to others while they work. These people may hole up and focus on their computers and devices. I am one of these people. I feel welcome with them too.

A few show up wanting only to talk. This is harder for me. I feel less welcome with them. But as the person running the space, I had to adapt to make them feel welcome. I learned to clear most of my Wednesdays for the people who show up—any people—so that I can work with them, talk with them, show up for what they need. I've learned to feel more welcome with the chatty as a result.

A few people show up expecting others to have created amazing community for them and to take advantage of the amazing community already here without becoming part of the community itself. I feel decidedly unwelcome with them. These people teach me some of the most important lessons I've learned in the space. In the CD, depending on who we are, we might call these people privileged or gentrifiers or sales people or non-resident developers or assholes or friends. I know this now, because I know I have been most of these things myself at some point—I came blindly into the neighborhood myself and could do that because I'm white. I know us when I see us. A couple of people have shown up disappointed in us from beginning to end. For example, they showed up on a day where there were only two of us here at the time, and I can only assume the community didn't look or feel as big, abundant or welcoming as they expected. Instead of staying to create community together, they spoke only to express concern and wouldn't engage with me at all (and so couldn't know how amazing the community here actually is and I couldn't know how amazing they are either). They didn't notice community members' photos on the walls behind them, stayed a short time, never came back, and never told us why. It may or may not surprise you, friends, that these were all white people. I learned to be ok with this too. The people who come back to our home—people who recognize that we create the community we want by showing up and putting our butt in the seat beside neighbors and working together—are those I ultimately want to work with anyway. The unwelcome-from-beginning-to-end folks taught me to make peace with feeling unwelcome, and I will never forget the lessons they taught me and the mirror they held up to me about how clueless I myself used to be and often still am.

Twice someone showed up unable or unwilling to bend themselves to fit into what was happening the day they happened to show up—and uninterested in talking to us about how we could bend to accommodate them. This is hard. Did I make them feel unwelcome somehow? Could I have done better? I'm learning to let this be hard. To accept I can't feel welcome to everyone.

A few people (three in the 2 years I ran our space) showed up skeptical that in-home co-working works. They were either vocally skeptical (2) or quietly skeptical (1). This makes me feel unwelcome and I learned to let them be skeptical. Coworking, or just our space, may be the wrong place for them. If so, being skeptical is the smart move for them. Trying to change their minds is a waste of time/breath and doesn't honor their gut instincts. They're welcome to leave or to stay and learn to make coworking work together, for ourselves, like the rest of us.

For me, the worst days were when nobody shows up at all. At first, this made me feel unwelcome. Eventually, instead of contemplating what a loser I am, I began using these days to focus on thinking about how to get a broader swath of our neighborhood walking in our doors or how to grow closer to those who came before. I learned to be humble here, alone, and I learned where I would need help if I was going to see the changes in the space I wanted to see. I also learned that cats and dogs are fantastic coworkers. Cats and dogs make me feel welcome. I also learned that I can make myself feel welcome on my own.

Our coworking space took something that I already thought was a good idea—regularly putting myself into positions to feel unwelcome so I'd better understand the experience of so many others—and made it my routine. I learned to leave my Wednesdays open to be available for those who didn't fit the norm of the day, whatever it happened to be that day. I learned to let the quiet focus as they needed to focus and to let the talkers talk when they wanted to talk. Running the space, I naturally learned how to wordlessly shift talkers into one room and hole-uppers into another room when that seemed called for, and others have learned that too. Today, as a member, I don't clear my schedule for others. I show up with work. Although I do still bend quite a bit as needed. We learn how to make ourselves feel welcome here, no matter what's happening from day to day. This is a community magic ninja skill.

# Hint 24: Practice running the space with full presence and without words.

Most days, people show up, settle in, figure out the norm of the moment, or day, and go with it. Like 6 different birds and 3 different fish becoming a flock/school and moving magically in sync. People are astonishing. Amazing.

When something happens that appears to be a disruption of the flow of the space, you have many choices. One option is to be bothered by a disruption yet do nothing. One option is not to be bothered and to try to do something about it. Another option is to be ok with a disruption, be silent, and do nothing about the disruption. Let it happen. See what other people need. See what other people do. Another option is joining the disruption and making it bigger. That can be really fun too.

BCS (before Collective Self), my go-to approach was to feel interruptions to my work as annoying disruptions. I used to try to fix situations that felt like disruptions. With time, I learned that joining disruptions is more fun and often what I personally need most at that moment. I eventually learned to leave my own work schedule more open on coworking Wednesdays to be available for disruption. Especially to be available for those who didn't fit the norm of the moment, or day, whatever it happened to be that moment/day. This always-focused-on-her-own-work writer learned how to be present for those in the space who need me present, at least part of the time. To sit and just listen to those who need to talk or vent or yell or cry. To join those who want to cook, or brainstorm, or play laser-chase (aka, Batman the cat). Full presence for someone is an amazing gift. I love receiving it. I'm still learning to give it. I'm remarkably, stubbornly devoted to the conversations and plans in my own head.

I also learned not to try being present for others when I can't be. Some days I'm legitimately busy, or tired, or sad, or in crisis, or I just stepped on a wasp with my bare foot, and I can't be present for others. I learned to let this be ok too. This is a community after all. I'm a member here, too, not the god of coworking.

Animals are great teachers of wordless presence. They let us be who we are by simply being ok with who they are. Like the day our neighbors Scott and Rachelle's chickens got out and came to coworking being chatty, fat, and adorable and making little nests for themselves in the newly applied wood mulch in the flowerbeds outside our windows and then gossiping about themselves and us even more once they'd settled in. We humans chatted far more that day ourselves—got considerably closer as a result. Chickens were our leaders. That was a fun day. I hated calling Rachelle to let her know they'd worked together and outsmarted their fence. For a bunch of individual silly chickens, wow are they smart together.

A final note for others like me: those compelled to be constantly offering help. Somebody needing constant help from you can feel like a disruption: most people get that. However, so can somebody constantly offering help. As if we're the only one in the space competent enough to see that help is needed and respond. That was the old Lori. I'm incredibly lucky that a few people (like Daniel, Chris, and Tim) put up with me long enough to allow me to figure this one out for myself.

## Hint 25: Put leadership in its place.

Running the space, I apparently began my own internal process of unlearning my definitions and expectations of leadership. I remembered—for good this time—that leadership looks and feels different to everyone and even different moment to moment for us as individuals.

I apparently used to think that leadership meant feeling responsible for others all the time. Because that's how I felt at the beginning—responsible for everybody else's experience in the space. Some of that is inevitable, I think, if it's your home the space is in. At least for me as a woman. I felt responsible for how others experienced our home. I don't anymore. Well, a lot less than I did before. Today I know that people are capable and responsible for their own experiences. All people.

I learned to value people for who they are in the moment: to let someone inclined to be quiet focus as she needs to focus and to let talkers talk when they want to talk. To let silly people be silly. To let angry people be angry. To let cooks be cooks and activists be activists and dogs be dogs. I began taking a more conscious, active role in the hardest task of all: allowing me to be me.

Batman helped. I learned to stop apologizing for Batman the cat being Batman back when he and I ran the space and he was a kitten. One day I just stopped. So a frisky black cat drops a laser pointer in your lap, or jumps in your bag, every few hours. That was part of working here back then. Batman showed up every day and was devoted to bringing more play into our community. Why did I think it was my job to stop him? Ultimately I learned that others and Batman could work out their own work/play arrangements for themselves 99.999% of the time. I learned that most people felt my interference and apologies as the disruption, not his playfulness. (Note: Batman moved to Whidbey when I did—talk about a devoted community member. Currently cats Teo and Spice run the coworking space. They are older than Batman and don't insist on play quite as aggressively as he did. They also don't chew on Tim's wool socks all the time, like Joey Big Paws did. They're charming hosts.)

Different moments need different leaders. Occasionally that's me. Running the space taught me a new citizenship-leadership: be present enough to honor the values and needs of the space and the moment.

I also learned a mountain of things I didn't know I was learning. For example, I learned how to wordlessly shift and take a too-loud talker into another room with me, if everybody else is stiffening, showing discomfort, or giving silent death glares. And if everyone is talking, and one person clearly needs silence and is mentally struggling with the decision about what to do, I might shift into another room and go silent myself, giving wordless permission for them to follow and do the same. I also learned when not to do these things: to allow others to lead the space silently too. I do this intuitively now and almost, but not quite, unconsciously. I didn't fully realize when I choose to do this, and choose not to, until months after Nicole took over running the space and I saw other people doing this really well too. Now I prefer to wait and watch what other Jedi's do most days. This is a practice of community Jedi masters—to feel the room, feel the space between us, know the strengths of those around them, and either act just a tiny bit—subtly—when really needed, or not act at all when somebody else would do better in the active role.

My leadership practice today: to stay present enough to notice how amazing everyone around me is. When I can't do that, to at least stay present enough to notice how capable and brave we all are.

## Hint 26: Offer outside-your-comfort-zone alternatives to your space.

Those of us who work nomadically are usually thrilled to learn about other options in the area—either because we like to float around or because we need more community. Often both. So we tend to share other options as a matter of habit. This hint is more than that.

When you run a coworking space, begin visiting even more spaces. As you visit other spaces, remember the people in those spaces, how they welcome people, and notice who felt welcome there, especially when you didn't. When someone comes into your space and doesn't feel welcome—no matter what any of you do—honor that person as a neighbor and offer them alternative spaces in the area. Depending on the person, it could be other coworking spaces, artist spaces, maker spaces, libraries, dance clubs, restaurants, museums, community centers, coffee shops, parks, shelters, rallies, for-rent private office space, or gardens, for example.

As a person running a space, to be truly useful to a wide variety of others, you have to be willing to walk into a wide variety of spaces, especially places where you yourself don't automatically feel welcome. Places, for example, where you are the only member of your gender or color or size or age group or sexual orientation or religious affiliation or political affiliation. You have to be willing to go places that scare you. This is entirely you-dependent. What is scary for you might be the opera, or a police station, or a store or restaurant where nobody speaks English or where English is the only language spoken, or a playground filled with kids, or a hospital. Might be a human-rights or worker-rights protest. Or a church, temple, or mosque. Or an elder-care home. Or a city council meeting.

You might not feel welcome there. But others do. Our in-home community spaces will never be all things to all people: they can't be. If you have alternatives at the ready, then even if somebody leaves your space and never comes back, you've honored them enough to offer them something of value to them as they go. You've been a good neighbor.

## Hint 27: Reimagine security and safety.

Yes, this one is long. This is important to me. Deal.

Many of the trappings of safety and security in our old at-work worlds—for example, locked doors, video cameras, metal detectors, security guards, bars on windows, and weapons—don't make us feel safe long term. Some of us learn to feel unsafe in their absence. Some of us learn to feel remarkably unsafe in their presence. If these things made us feel truly safe as whole communities, I don't think we'd have any safety concerns about turning our homes into coworking or other community spaces now: no matter who we are. But we do. At least in my country we do.

One of the things we're doing—just by turning our homes into community spaces for a few hours each week—is reinventing security and safety for ourselves. We're getting closer as neighbors and friends. We're facing our fears together. We're creating truly safe space for each other and for ourselves and for our neighbors. Opening a home as a coworking space—and showing up to work within one—means regularly inviting strangers into your personal space. This level of vulnerability can be scary at first. Awkward, at least. Because at the beginning you unlock that door—or walk in through it—having no guarantee that the community will create safe space for you. And if you're anything like 3-years-ago me, you may have little confidence that you have it in you to make a space feel safe for yourself, let alone for other people.

I was terrified the first few months I ran the space. What if a total asshole showed up? Like that guy at Microsoft who loudly dominated every meeting he was in to the point that everyone else tuned out completely and nobody got heard, including him? Or what if a criminal came in? I'd spent the majority of my career working in buildings with security systems, video cameras, security policies and procedures, and in some cases, security guards. I worked surrounded by people who'd been vetted, checked, and hired by in-charge others. All those things had made me feel safe in the moment, but they make more than half of the people in my community today feel unsafe, which really doesn't make any of us truly safer, does it? They also made me feel remarkably unsafe in their absence. Like I couldn't be safe without experts handling security for me. Then again, none of those things kept that total asshole off my Microsoft team. At the end of the day, it was still human beings and close relationships making us feel truly safe and secure most days.

Here in unlocked-front-door world, our ever-deepening and -expanding connections with those around us serve as safe-space generators. Those who show up and don't feel safe at all rarely show up, and when they do, they don't stay long, and they never come back. Most who show up and think "Nice, but not for me." are honored as neighbors and pointed to other spaces that are a better match for their energy or needs of the moment. Those who stay and create their own safety, connect quickly and feel safer for it, quickly. These connections are person-specific—everybody's community is slightly different from everybody else's. And relatively quickly, all these personally-trusted community fields begin to overlap and work together for the benefit of everyone in the coworking space, expanding outward into the neighborhood that holds you. Eventually, we moved outside our doors and into working elsewhere in the neighborhood together—taking our new-found small-group safety and security out with us and connecting ours with others doing the same.

And you won't take my word for it. Until you experience this regularly and reliably in your home space, you're going to be a little (or a lot) scared. So it's ok, in unlocked-front-door world, to start very small, humbly, and with people known to you and those around you. I started by inviting people I knew and by asking housemates and neighbors to do the same. Because I was going to be a lone woman, sitting in a house the same day/time each week, with an unlocked door, in a neighborhood best known by outsiders for drive-by shootings and drugs.

I under-advertised on purpose at first. I asked my new friends at Office Nomads and The Hub to send us only personal referrals for community members who really need our space and NOT to advertise in their newsletters and things. I didn't advertise in the neighborhood online newspaper right away either. Or do postcards or buttons or anything that could be physically spread around the neighborhood at first. All that came later: when the community created those things for itself. All I had at the start was our Facebook page, which had been my blogger/writer page before I gave it to the space, and everyone who had liked it back then knew me—or at least my writing—personally.

What the coworking space taught me is that I myself was an outsider in the Central District—until the coworking space and the people who walked in each week—changed me. Until the space taught me what the Central District really is. Who we are. What matters to us. And how freaking amazing the people in the neighborhood actually are—each moment we drop our fears, come together, and experience it.

I won't sugar coat this for you. Becoming your own personal and neighborhood security system is totally fucking amazing. And hard at first. And then less hard. And then a lot less hard than I thought it would be. One day I couldn't fully remember why I thought this would be hard for me/us. In-home coworking and community spaces are not the locked-door world: not while coworking is happening anyway. They are bridge spaces in that way. I think they exist to teach us something else, something new. In them, we learn how to be our own security systems. And we learn how to be total community bad asses together—at least people like me who'd forgotten that we could be.

The other cool part is that we hang on to what we learn and take it with us wherever we go. As an individual, I'm disinclined to settle for less everywhere I go now. In groups, I look around and see who is feeling unsafe, and I support them however I can. And I speak up whenever I feel unsafe—sometimes in the moment, sometimes the next day after I've collected my thoughts. In part, to demonstrate that it's ok to speak up for your own safety. And safe to do so with me. For example, in some of my online discussions—where I am often the only woman present—when I feel unsafe, I say so now. In arguments with extended family, when I feel unsafe, I say so. If I feel intensely unsafe with someone, I won't stay in their presence. In three years, this has never happened to me in our coworking space. But it has happened to me with some of my own extended family members this past year. I told them I needed to walk away for a year and come back when I feel safe again. This, too, is new for me.

Here in our new Whidbey neighborhood, at a 60ish-person community meeting last summer, when one neighbor (who only lives here 3 months out of the year) suggested that we get video cameras pointing at all the shared spaces for security purposes, I was brave enough to speak up, share our Collective Self story with all the new neighbors here I knew, and speak my own perspective—namely that, for me, neighbors getting closer makes us more secure and video cameras, which advertise both financial wealth and community absence, are more likely to draw crime to neighborhoods than prevent it. Building-mounted video cameras pointed at me make me feel unsafe. I am a neighbor. My experience and my voice counts—no matter how much of an outsider I appear to be.

No need to agree with me on security and safety specifics. My point is that the in-home community space itself has made me a lot more aware, stronger, braver, more vocal, more empathetic, more inclined to listen deeply to those present, more able to help myself and others feel safe, and more heard as an individual. Three years ago, I wouldn't have had the courage to share my perspective with brand new neighbors decades older than me—especially men and especially in a legacy neighborhood like this one where almost everyone else is fourth and fifth generation family, while Daniel and I are outsiders and brand new. Frankly, three years ago I didn't have enough awareness about the subject of safety and security to know the specifics of my own perspective, because somebody else had always handled work security and safety for me.

I used to think I couldn't handle safety and security for myself. Now I can and I do. With everyone I meet. In thousands of small invisible little ways and occasionally in a louder way.

Backed by an always-expanding community, I've become a mobile safe-space generator. Safe space moves with me now. I continue making choices each day to handle safety and security for myself and to ask those I'm with to do the same—often without words or in the tiniest of moments—which means I get a little better at this every day now too. So do those I'm with.

This is no small thing.

Here in Lori Land, this is a game changer.

Hint 28: Notice that listening to what is needed by everyone has become a habit.

People interested in changing yourself, the neighborhood, or the world, this tip is for you. Listening to the community, to neighbors, or to yourself once is simple. Why is it so freakishly hard to do these things long term, day in and day out?

Here regularly listening to what the neighborhood needs doesn't feel hard anymore, most days. Most days, it's dead simple. The neighborhood walks in the door and talks about what it wants. Some days, we go out and ask. Both approaches just became a habit along the way.

Today when I say "here" what I mean is both in the coworking space and everywhere I go now. I've become a walking listening, recording, and sharing device. The habits I picked up running the space have stuck. I can't turn them off now. It's kind of awesome.

Hint 29: Notice that you've turned learning about neighborhood history into a habit.


We were interested in neighborhood history long before we opened our home as a co-working space. We managed to luck into buying a home between two community legends. Pastor Alice and family lived just to our north. Love them. You couldn't ask for better neighbors. They literally help everyone they meet. It's stunning. Now that we've moved away, I miss their kindness, laughter, generosity of spirit, and jazz wafting out on summer nights from their upstairs windows.

Charlie lived just to our south. He'd lived in the neighborhood since the 1940s, had long since retired from his job with the city, and neighborhood stories poured generously out of him like fine wine in the hands of a friend. I don't know how many years he taught Sunday school, but I'd guess at least 700.

One of our favorite Charlie stories is that back when he worked for the city, he'd plant seedling trees in the parking strip in front of his house, only to come home after work to find neighborhood trouble-making kids had broken them in half, killing them. So when he retired, he planted new trees, and then he sat on his front porch and watched the trees and the kids—for years—to make sure they'd all make it. This story was so powerful that Charlie has been gone 10 years now and neighbors up and down the block are still protecting each other, and his trees. Five years ago, when the city hired a not-great company to do street-tree trimming—and we saw them horribly topping tree after tree a few blocks away and leaving lush blocks looking like war zones—we leapt into action. Neighbor Annie—the woman who Charlie's family sold his house to after he passed because of her own stories of visiting family in the neighborhood—had her attorney boyfriend at the time draft a letter. We ran outside and tapped copies of the letter to both of Charlie's trees. The letter demanded that the trees not be touched until we got to talk with the city. It worked. They invited us to a community-wide meeting about neighborhood street-tree trimming and every single citizen who showed up in the room—somewhere between 10 and 15 of us—was there for one reason: to protect Charlie's trees. Annie even brought her own arborist. The city guys—who'd given a long speech about why what they were doing and how they were doing it was important—were stunned when they figured out that everyone in the room was there to protect the same two trees. We didn't even have to say anything. They allowed Annie's own arborist to trim Charlie's trees and said they wouldn't touch the trees for at least 2 years. That was a really good day.

All neighbors tell good stories, but we receive so much more than that now. Reimagining our home as a community space brought neighborhood history in through our doors on a regular basis, well beyond what we ever expected. For example, we got to become friends with John, a long-time CD neighbor who gives neighborhood history walks and helps with Hopscotch CD. One day Madeleine walked into coworking to commiserate with me as a fellow community story wrangler. She eventually added our story to her amazing The People of the Central Area and Their Stories blog/website. Check it out. It's amazing. Madeline has arranged for these stories to go to the Seattle Public Library after she's done with the work—for future generations. Thanks to her, I got to watch our story become history. Amazing. Now that I've moved away, I still hear about neighborhood history, and thanks to John, Madeline, Danyale, Knox, Jean, and many others, I always will.

# Hint 30: Be prepared for magic.

The first person to walk into our space the week we opened (besides me and the executive staff of cats and dog) was another community story wrangler! I'd never met another me! He told me about his project in which he and friends set up a table on their busy urban corner and gather/write neighbor's stories. He said "I just love to learn and love to be surrounded by learners." At the time, "loving to learn" was the thing I looked for in new friends and work colleagues. And this stranger just walked in my front door and said that out loud to me. How cool is that? I felt like hugging him as he left but didn't. I'd just met him. I didn't want to weird out the first stranger who showed up. Thanks Michael!

A year later another community story wrangler—at the time, a stranger—showed up. Both Madeleine, and her People of the Central Area blog, are beyond lovely. She showed up to gather our story—I couldn't believe it. It was the first time I'd ever been on the receiving end of community story wrangling. It was so powerful to get to tell our story—and the story of the expanding circles of amazing community we kept encountering together in the CD—that I was brought to tears in the telling. I did hug her as she left. And I've hugged her many times since. Thank you Madeleine!

Less than a year after that, another stranger walked in the door, worried because they'd found asbestos in her apartment's ductwork and she and her partner were going to have to find a place to move. An hour later, I knew that they'd be moving into our home, and taking over running the coworking space from me. This was beyond awesome. And honestly, by this point, not surprising. Our community is so over-lappy and cross-connected at this point, and so giving, that perfect-for-us others regularly show up, literally, at our front door. Thank you, Nicole, from the bottom of my heart, for making the home and space and neighborhood I love, ever more lovable.

Hugging strangers is a natural instinct for me now. I don't question my own instincts to hug people or play with people anymore. Magic tends to pop up everywhere now. I feel like a 44-year-old child. This makes all my relationships better. Interestingly, on the flip side, when I feel unsafe, I KNOW something is really wrong now. I don't question it. I do something about it closer to immediately now (depending on how unsafe I feel). I have removed myself from the presence of dangerous-for-me family members and friends this past year—not easy, but necessary. I didn't know I had that in me. I feel like running an in-home coworking space for a couple of years—and working on projects outside together in the neighborhood—gave me dog-like intuition. Being discerning and intuitive isn't as ruff now. ;-)

Because I speak so often of magic, sometimes people, including a couple of my friends and family members, think that I'm overly optimistic, naïve, or somehow blind to the problems of the world. Or that I live in a tiny little bubble of awesomeness in an otherwise horrible world. I make peace with that. We each see the world we create for ourselves first. And my world—wherever I go now—is full of wonder, mystery, magic, kind strangers, and people showing up to help and working to make things better. I don't mind walking into painful situations as much as I once did, because I have the sustained energy and confidence now to do so. In my world, this doesn't make me optimistic. This makes me able to be fully present and contributing where change is needed most and I am needed most. I don't apologize for what I am anymore. I don't ask others to either. If you happen to see me and I'm crying, don't bother worrying about me. That's just magic. It's everywhere in my world now and it tends to make my eyes water.

## Hint 31: Field trips!

When I ran our space, I was also a member of Office Nomads, and I occasionally went on their field trips with them. Nicole has taken this a step further for our space. She arranges field trips for coworkers here. Such a good idea. Women in their 20s rock.

So this Nicole-inspired tip is to arrange an occasional coworking day—or part of a day—to be a field trip somewhere else.

Nicole's done this three ways that I know of, likely many more. She arranged a trip to work/play in somebody else's home for the day. She arranged a visit to a nearby coworking space. And she arranged an afternoon trip to just fully relax together to better enjoy a rare moment (in our case, to a beach, to soak in that rarest of all things—a hot Seattle summer day).

To pull in more people of all ages and job types to join field trips, if you can, plan ahead and provide at least a couple weeks' notice, then a day-before notice, and then a morning-of notice.

To pull current community members closer—try smaller, spontaneous trips during the day for coffee or lunch and for drinks, dinner, or movies when coworking is over. Stick a note on the door and tell people to come join you where you went. Chuck's CD Hop Shop around the corner, where we're allowed to bring dogs with us to hang out after coworking, is our new best friend.

Hint 32: When enough people aren't showing up, grow closer to those who do show up.

Just because you offer your home as a free community space, doesn't necessarily mean you'll be flooded by people clamoring to join you. If you are, please email me and tell me your secret. For us, community creation and re-creation is fun, and it also takes considerable time and effort. The space never stops teaching us that community creation is ongoing, never-ending, and well worth it.

At the beginning, our in-home space—because it was already being paid for by our incomes and renters—took much of the pressure off me as an individual to push my ideas/work/services onto others that'd I'd been feeling before then as an independent worker. It allowed me to move in the world as more of a pull space, which I think must be closer to my own nature, because it pisses me off when people feel like they're pushing their work/ideas/services onto me. Bleh.

I didn't ever advertise in the CD News. But eventually Tom—its editor at the time, Hi Tom—stopped in to cowork with us. He encouraged me to write a story about ourselves in this community news outlet and even showed me how. Lately, Tom's been getting noticed more and more as a leader in Seattle thanks in part to his amazing work with the Seattle Bike Blog. Go Tom!

Our space showed up several times in the CD News after Tom's first visit—as stories, not ads. First, when Grady dog got lost and we were in a crazy panic to find him. Next, just to tell neighbors about our existence. Later, to periodially announce ourselves as a location for Hopscotch CD planning/crafting/creation meetings. That was fun.

Tabitha and I became friends early on, and one day our conversation led us create some postcards/fliers for the space to drop into Central Cinema, Katy's, Tougo Coffee, Earl's, 20/20 Cycle, and Cortona—the closest area businesses at the time. That was fun. I even got to pay Tabitha a little for her work—also fun. I spend a lot of time telling people about Tabitha's art and work and where it's available because she's amazingly talented and burdened with a soul-deep dislike of marketing for herself. I know the feeling. We also took our homemade products to Backyard Barter sessions. More fun. She now creates marketing materials, covers, and illustrations for our books. And mostly we're just friends. Life and gardening gurus for each other. She's a gift beyond measure.

During Hopscotch CD event planning/creating, word of our space spread far wider. Neighbors gathered here and we made "I Love the CD" buttons and a hundred painted hopscotch rocks for the event. That was fun. I fell in love with dozens of neighbors thanks to that event.

Nicole hasn't advertised the space either, that I know of. She's been using dinners and field trips and tea to get closer to the community already here. Hosting an at-home, on-the-couch film festival brought new folks in too.

Hint 33: Protect the crap out of your time (aka, learning to say no to dear friends).

Running a space eventually meant that I had exponentially more friends across my own neighborhood and the surrounding neighborhoods than I'd ever had before. These are people who I love, who loved the idea of community coworking, love me, and see potential in me that I don't see in myself. Which is amazing, right? Yes and.

Exponentially more people were now asking me to join them, get involved, and not just get involved but take on leadership roles. This wasn't like my old day-job world, where saying "No" was easier because I didn't like half the people asking things of me. Here, literally everybody who asks me to do things with them is someone I respect and admire, if not love so much that I'm compelled to hug them every time I see them. I had to learn to regularly say no to awesome people doing awesome things or my head would have exploded.

I sound like a total tool in this message from three years back: I was still way too close to my doctoral dissertation years to sound like a normal human. But I share it here to demonstrate what I mean...

"Hi Chelsea, I'm going to say 'thank you, and no' to your generous invitation to have me on the [Seattle Collaborative Space Alliance] board. The truth is, I hear the words 'President, Vice President, Treasurer, and Secretary' and I feel no energy for the idea of being part of that. Words matter to me, and these words suck energy for me, carrying the baggage of hierarchical organizational systems in their pairing. I believe that formal organizational systems exist for those who need them, as they should. I'm just not one of those people. So happy to host, gather stories, advise, support, celebrate, promote, and otherwise party it up in support of your efforts. But no to formal membership. Thanks!! Lori"

Good God I used a lot of big words back then. I'm amazed I had any friends at all. It's a damn good thing for me that I was living in over-educated Seattle. ;-)

# Hint 34: Expect to begin standing up for your neighborhood. A lot.

At some point near the end of my first year in our space, I began being regularly feisty enough to speak up whenever I thought the needs of the Central District weren't being considered or the value of our neighborhood wasn't being fully understood. Not that I understand everything myself—I'm often queen of the clueless. But I do understand the value of this neighborhood and the communities and history it holds. I understand what hurts our neighbors now: at least well enough to know when to involve myself in the conversation. In my first 10 years in the CD, I'd rarely had the courage to speak up. Frankly, combining full-time work with full-time school meant I wasn't out in the neighborhood enough to have the first clue about when I should speak up or what I should say.

Less than a year into running our in-home space, I found myself speaking up often, instinctively and with minimal fear around neighbors and friends, as if it was something I'd always done and was naturally good at. A year and a half in, I was speaking about the needs of the neighborhood in rooms full of strangers outside the space. More importantly, I was speaking to my friends about our needs.

For example. This is an excerpt from an email I sent to a dear friend in the Seattle Collaborative Space Alliance, back when the alliance was considering adding a $100 annual membership fee to be a member space in the alliance...

"Girl, I know you'd break a rule in a heartbeat. It's not Collective Self coworking (our space) I was thinking of. I'm not worried about us, we're great. And we have money. My perspective on an amount of money as an entry fee [for Seattle Collaborative Space Alliance] has everything to do with the neighborhood we sit in—the history of this place speaks to me. And the knowledge that the moment you make money your entry criteria, you keep a whole lot of awesome out. It's just a question of what do we want to see more of in SCSA in the coming year or two? For me it would be diversity, differences celebrated, creativity, and fun. I think we need more "Hey, we're silly!" than "Hey, we're serious!" Perhaps that's just me. I've personally got truckloads of serious. I need more silly. – Lori"

When I see the need to speak up now, I speak up. Sometimes quietly, like this, and sometimes loudly. I've pointed out to people at UW the absurdity of not even having my neighborhood as a choice in their online survey. The blind act of making the CD invisible will not stand in my presence. God that burns me. Our universities have come a long way. And wow do they have a long way to go. I've written letters of frustration to Seattle Tilth—a wildly popular urban gardening non-profit for whom I've done volunteer work over the years—saying that although I would love to, I won't involve myself in their Master Composter program until they figure out a way for it to be free or far more affordable for low-income city residents. In countless little moments of my life, I now make a choice to speak up, share a little neighborhood history here, a little neighborhood present-day reality there. I don't know which part I think is cooler: the fact that I'm actually able to speak up now or the fact that I can see when I need to. This makes me feel more alive, awake, and more fully human. And I have Collective Self Coworking and the Central District to thank for that.

I know these are small things. I just happen to believe deeply in the power of small things.

Hint 35: Fall in love with neighborhood sounds. Change the sounds nobody can live with.

The CD is full of amazing sounds. She taught me to love the sounds within parades and protests and rallies and street carnivals and street musicians. The sounds within distant marching bands practicing in parks. The sound of downtown's trains wafting up to us in the middle of the night. I fell in love with the sound of neighbors teasing and yelling to each other across the street. The sound of kids playing in the street during block parties. The sound of busy white guys talking into ear pieces as they walk by and groups of teenage girls laughing and collective-advice-giving into their phones. I adjusted to the stream of ambulance sirens heading to Pill Hill, where most of Seattle's hospitals live. I grew accustomed to the airplanes overhead: even the Blue Angels who rattled our windows every August and sent our cats sprawling flat under beds. I love the way that the chickens in neighbors' backyards sound like groups of old ladies gossiping. I love the sounds of camaraderie and family emanating outward from churches, Earl's barbershop, and Danyale's Good Hair Salon. I even enjoy the sound of loudly bickering couples walking down the middle of the street yelling at each other during a fight. To have the courage to be that open with my marital dirty laundry in public. Wow. Maybe someday. I love the sounds of neighbors in backyards, on front porches, and working in our space.

Two of her sounds I never got used to.

Gunfire is not an uncommon sound in the CD, and I refuse to get used to it. Every time I hear it I imagine a young kid dying. Every single time. I'm not alone in this. This is not a sound to get used to or fall in love with. This is a sound to do something about as a community.

The sound of squealing tires in car collisions or near misses is also not uncommon in the CD. Many people driving cars race through our neighborhood from their jobs downtown to their homes in neighborhoods to the east of us. There aren't nearly enough safe options for people walking and riding bikes, and you can hear it. I never want to get used to the sound of car collisions. There aren't enough people fighting for the rights of residents who live in the CD to feel safe crossing busy streets, let alone having beautiful community-enriching passageways for people on foot and on bikes.

I'm not alone in this either. This is a sound to do something about as a community.

# Hint 36: Expect to become someone new.

Some days running an in-home coworking space is hard. Once somebody showed up who thought the idea of in-home coworking was a stupid idea and spent an hour telling me why. Once somebody showed up who wouldn't stop asking personal questions of people who'd already established that they'd like several hours of quiet that day to get some work done. The worst days, though, were the days nobody showed up and I coworked with my cat, feeling like a loser, and having to make peace with that. Some days it was hard. And I chose it anyway.

The space eventually stretched me enough that I left my comfort zone, joined neighbors, and began working to make our neighborhood a closer, even more welcoming place.

One day I found myself saying things that I didn't have the courage to say out loud and talking with people I wasn't strong enough to speak to. For example, defending our plan to create a 2-mile hopscotch-path-centered event to 25 different city officials at once—from the department of transportation to economic development to police to parks and recreation to special events. I'd come home at night thinking "Who the hell was that? I'm not brave enough to do that."

I found myself leaving home to join more neighborhood gatherings and meetings that made me feel uncomfortable, occasionally unsafe. I noticed that my white skin is a kind of shield and that some people live with this unsafe feeling every day of their lives, while I usually get to choose it. So I began choosing to be in places where self-expansion wouldn't be an option for me anymore. I step into discomfort now. It's part of being a good neighbor.

Sometimes I find myself standing in the presence of unimaginable personal pain with strangers. Crying together. Showing up to help those fighting for better community—people in tents or carrying signs, bringing their pain out into the open for the world to see. With neighbors I realized that I can do the same thing. I eventually learned that my fear wasn't about "them" (strangers, aka, people I don't recognize as part of my community). My fear and associated anger were about me: about my own inability to handle them. Or, more specifically, to handle those parts of me—the lost, frustrated, mistreated, angry, overlooked, attacked, forgotten, silent, and strange. I can handle more parts of me now, which means there's more and more "us" and less and less "them." You don't scare me. I scare me. And I'm learning to live with that and change it.

I learned that I have way more resources around me and within me than I ever imagined. That we have it within us to forge ourselves and our neighborhoods anew.

Why did I think I didn't have it in me to do this?

Why did I believe there was nothing I could do to tackle the hardest problems in my own neighborhood?

Why did I make decision after decision that kept me from getting closer to people in my own neighborhood and community?

I can't tell you why. I can't remember that me anymore.

## Hint 37: Did I mention magic? Let's mention it again, shall we?

Thanks to our years reimagining our home as a collaborative space today we have friends and community across the Central District neighborhood, across many neighborhoods in Seattle, across collaboration-centered spaces in the region, on Bainbridge and Whidbey islands, and in coworking spaces and large-scale hopscotch event creators in other parts of the world.

We've made friends with people within city government and with people changing government from the outside.

Friends with cops who stop by for neighborhood picnics and friends with people who hate cops.

Friends with local small business owners, local large commercial-land owners, and people who run local non-profits. We're friends with neighborhood legends and treasures. Happy birthday Jean!

Friends with several homeless men who fully demonstrated that courage and community building have nothing to do with money.

I'm friends with many parents in the neighborhood, even though I have no children and I once thought we had nothing in common.

We even finally became cool enough—visibly doing good with people across the neighborhood—to make friends in the CD's black community beyond our next door neighbors Alice and Charlie. BTW, thank you, Pastor Alice. And rest in peace, Charlie. Thank you so much for long lifetimes of giving to this community and for the amazing families you brought into the world. Good neighbors are a blessing beyond measure.

As a writer, it's relatively easy for me to make friends in the online world but making friends in person isn't easy for me at all. I'm quiet. Don't like small talk. Prefer writing to speaking. Today, because of our little space, I'm friends with hundreds of people, some of whom cowork at the CD house, many of whom are friends, and many of whom now show up on Whidbey at our new home 90 minutes away. The space moves with me.

I made some dear friends during my twenty years working in the corporate and academic worlds—but nothing remotely close to this. I carry this space within me. And I return regularly, so I get to watch a new generation change the space for themselves. Change the neighborhood we all love for the better. It's amazing what this little community coworking space does. It makes me feel like the luckiest human on earth.

Working in the Space

## Hint 38: Be a bit fluid with your personal space and personal plans

This is Tim's hint. He's been a coworker extraordinaire since the week we began more than 3 years ago.

A home is a personal, intimate space. An in-home work space can't not be about community. It can't not be intimate. At least for us. This can be a bit weird, especially at first. In the part of the world where our space is, many of us are accustomed to working in impersonal spaces, so a lot of what we consider "normal" for a work environment, I think, is based on our experience working in impersonal spaces.

Personal space example
At the big round 10-person table, if there are three of us here, we naturally spread out. Sometimes a 4th and 5th person show up, so we shift, making space for them. When a 6th person shows up, we shift a little again. And we just keep on shifting a little bit as things change. This happens fluidly, without people being told when or how to shift. We just do. If a lot of people want to work at the big table, some of us who can work in any position shift into the living room. Or we move between spaces every hour or two just to mix things up. Sometimes people are even working on the kitchen and living room floors — workshop planning or making physical things or playing with a cat. Or drawing at the kitchen counter. Or sticking flip chart paper to the windows during brainstorming. Sometimes people cook or bake. Jane and Nicole have been known to go upstairs and cowork/co-snuggle with Eva dog on the bed. It's a warm, mostly comfortable chaos, and for those who choose to work here, it always just works out somehow. To me it feels like magic.

Personal plans example
Yesterday Tim shared this random story about the "ape index" which has something to do with your height in inches, length of your arm span in inches, and our evolution. Without even knowing exactly why, we all suddenly leapt up and began measuring arm spans and heights to figure out ape index numbers for each other. For the pure fun of it. Small shifts in personal plans happen all the time here. A group decides to go for a walk. A few people walk to get coffee or lunch. Someone asks for 5 minutes of input and we all brainstorm together for a few minutes on their issue. Once Forrest showed up wanting to test-run his jokes before he went on stage to do stand-up comedy that night – and we got a free 30-minute stand-up comedy show at the end of our work day. Some people—like Tim, like me—make sure that almost all of our personal work plans can shift on coworking Wednesday, so that no matter who shows up or what others need, at least one person is present and available for them. You don't have to be this flexible. We do it because it's fun for us and because we can.

**Hint 39: If you have specific needs for the day, tell people what your needs are for that day.**

Crap, this is either Nicole or Jane or Susan's hint, I can't remember which. Let's just thank them all, shall we?

Even for those of us accustomed to the warm, comfortable chaos of coworking here most days, sometimes chaos doesn't work.

If you show up and need two solid hours of quiet to meet a deadline, tell us that. If you need help with brainstorming for 30 minutes, tell us that. It's easy enough to make one room the mostly quiet room and one room the talking room. If you'd like to bring a client in and have a 2-hour meeting and reserve the whole living room for yourself, tell us that, preferably ahead of time. If your head will explode if you don't get to bake cake pops in the kitchen, tell us that. If you want everyone in the coworking space to go on a field trip somewhere else for the day, tell us that.

And if it's really, really, really important to you to get exactly what you need on a particular day, try warning us ahead of time via the Facebook page or Twitter or email or text or whatever works at reaching your coworkers here. For example, Nicole used the Facebook page to move coworking to Whidbey Island for a day and to arrange a field trip to another space one week. I recently used the Facebook page and my own Twitter account to tell people a week in advance, a day in advance, and then same day, that I wanted to pick their brains for this section of the book. And poof—10 people showed up to help me in February.

## Hint 40: If our space doesn't work for you, before you go, ask about other options.

This is Susan and Lori's hint. Susan is a neighbor who occasionally works or plays in our space or drops Buckley dog off so he can babysit the humans. She's also founder/owner/operator of Office Nomads, an amazing coworking space in Capitol Hill, an adjoining neighborhood.

The personal, informal, intimate experience of coworking here in our home doesn't work for everybody, and we're fine with that. It doesn't hurt our feelings if you try it and don't like it, or never come back. Before you go, consider spending a couple of minutes talking to one of us about what you do want in a work space, because we are literally brimming with other options. There are hundreds of people and spaces we're connected to now. Don't leave without taking advantage of the awesomeness that is us. Here are some of the options you have:

- Ask if you can try something else with our space. For example, Tabitha created Saturday crafternoons here because for her to find coworking appealing, we had to be making things together. Fisher used the space one Monday evening/month for his facilitator's meetup group. Neither comes to coworking Wednesdays, but both connected in their own ways, and remain connected to us as friends today. Or ask if we can try something different one Wednesday, such as a field trip, or quiet working for 45 minutes and talking for 15 minutes all day, instead of the more random way we normally do things.

- Go try one of the several dozen other coworking spaces in the area. We're connected to many of them and are happy to recommend specific spaces and people, based on your needs. In Seattle, if you visit five Seattle Collaborative Space Alliance spaces, you win a really cool space traveler mug for boldly going where few others have gone before. We're cool like that.

- Go try one of the several dozen other alternative work spaces in the area. We're nomadic humans and workers too. We all know details about and people at area coffee shops, libraries, community centers, back nooks or rooms of bookstores, parks – you name it, one of us has worked there. We have details about noise level, WiFi strength, cool people, food, coffee, etc.

- Turn your own home or space into another coworking space. Run it the way you want it run. Nothing makes Lori happier than hearing about this.

Leaving without talking to us about what you want is a mistake from our perspective. Because what if—God forbid—you leave thinking that you suck at coworking, or worse, that we do! ;-) From our perspective, you leaving doesn't mean that any of us suck at coworking. Leaving means that we're all masters of moving around to get our work-space and community needs met. Masters of going where we're most needed.

# Hint 41: Try leading with "How can I contribute?"

This is Susan's hint. Congrats on your new itty bitty coworker, Susan, and on your gaggle of new baby chickens!

I love this hint. In their space, Susan's noticed that people who show up asking themselves "What can I give to this community?" or "How can I contribute?" end up happier, staying longer, making more friends and connections, etc. than people who show up leading with the question "What can this community do for me?"

Hearing her say this, I recognized that this is true in our little space too. Those who stay, or stay connected, are those who willingly give to the community. Those who see what they have to offer as valuable, no matter how small or weird (ape index!), and experience themselves as a vital community member. Those who experience a direct connection between the success of the community and their success as an individual (or group or organization or neighborhood or city).

The other people working in and running a space can tell us we're valuable—vital—to the success of the space and the community, and even try to show us how much we matter. But nobody can make us see this. We have to experience it for ourselves. Today, the best way I know how to get to that personally experienced feeling of being vital to a community is to contribute—to give something: a coffee-shop recommendation, an idea about how to grow better vegetables, a tip about the best route for someone on a bike to get somewhere, cookies you made yourself, a library book recommendation, or 5 minutes of your time to brainstorm on somebody else's project.

## Hint 42: If you stay, prepare to be wow'd. And loved.

From my perspective, people who show up willing to be a bit fluid with their personal space and personal plans—and spend even half a day working fluidly with others doing the same—tend fall in love with us rapidly, and we with them, almost instantly.

These new people tend to make friends quickly and become connectors for each other quickly too, exponentially expanding each other's communities in very smart, efficient, I-know-you-and-what-you-want and I-know-the-exact-perfect-person-for-you-to-talk-to kinds of ways.

We tend to fall in love with each other and the space simultaneously. And I don't use love lightly. People who become friends/members (here if you come back for a second time you are automatically a member of the space) love and are loved by at least one person here, if not by everyone here. And it usually happens fast. Like love at first sight, only love at first visit. Visit the Collective Self page on Facebook to feel the love from a distance.

# Hint 43: Prepare to be needed.

We are a tiny space. Across three years, I'd guess maybe 200 people have become members. Members are people who show up in person more than once and opt to stay connected by continuing to work here, by doing something else with the space (like hosting a game night or birthday party or evening salon etc.), and by becoming friends.

Most people who come into the coworking space are really busy. Busy people are needed—they often focus on their own work, so the space doesn't become too loud from talking.

Those who aren't busy—for example retired people, between-jobs people, people who clear time just to be present or to cook for us—are a huge gift too. Full presence is awesome and needed. And yay food.

To this day, on any given Wednesday, there are usually between 2 and 8 people coworking over the course of the day here. And it's different every week. On any given Wednesday, it could be just Nicole, one friend, plus cats Teo and Spice here when you show up, although others usually show up later. Every person who shows up is important to us and is needed by us to reimagine the space and become part of the story.

I feel so lucky to get 8 people in the door on Wednesdays. People's needs change with time. Some people only cowork in the summer. Many only when they're between day jobs. Some only once or twice a year. Some show up only to work with Nicole or me or someone else here. Many people work just part of the day here, not the whole day. Some just stop by to say hi or share news. Some stop by to learn about the space (yay neighbors and other new coworking space folks). Some just drop off hugs or supplies or treats to the space (yay Madeleine and Knox!). Neighbor Scotia—a friend of Lori's—comes by just to share tea, conversation, and read her mail. Or read a book. Some people only come when they're directly invited by one of their friends to work with them here. Some only showed up to work on a project like Hopscotch CD with us or to attend an after-hours event like an Impacts of Gentrification salon or a backyard BBQ or a Saturday crafternoon or a planning meeting.

If you walk in the door even once, you are needed here. Each time you come back, you make us feel needed too.

## Hint 44: Notice your impact on others.

What does your presence add? What does your leaving do? What happens when you share things? When you cook together? When you change your behavior? Experiment. If you do, you may find that you're more important than you think you are.

One approach to noticing is to ask about your impact to others. Simple, but not easy. And so worth it.

# Hint 45: Don't apologize for being yourself. Don't ask others to either.

I adore context and tend to be long-winded and wind in circles getting to the point on subjects I love. I'm not easy for get-to-the-point people. Friends call me wending.

I spend a lot of time alone, even when others are around, silent and lost within my own imagination. Friends recognize me as focused and hard-working, or spacey and a dreamer, or as a poet and writer.

I use the words wonder and awe and play and mystery and magic and pirate and mermaid and dragon more than most adults. I am a wanderer. Most days I love being lost. This can make me unpopular with people who'd prefer it if I grew up or lived in their version of the real world. I don't mind. My friends draw me dragons. See me do just fine in the real world most days.

I am short. You may have to reach things from high places for me. Friends call me a "road-trippers friend."

I cry when I am touched by what others are doing. Sometimes I cry when others and I are in pain. Or when something is so beautiful that words aren't good enough. My friends either love this or deal with this about me.

I am a dog and cat mom. I leave a wake of pet hair behind me. Often have my dog with me. My cat may insist you play with him by dropping laser pointers in your lap repeatedly. My other cat might seem oddly turned on by wool socks, especially when they have feet in them. Friends send me pet videos. Let me know when they'd prefer Eva dog be put outside or brought inside. Take drugs if they're allergic and want to sleep over.

When people complain for hours without moving into what they're doing about it, or talk technology details, my mind wanders. She apparently has better things to do. I'm not always the boss of her.

When people change things for themselves, my heart rejoices. I tell their stories a lot. It's hard to get me to shut up about it, actually.

I am straight and white and not religious in the traditional sense. No amount of gay friends and black friends and Asian friends and Hispanic friends and friends from other countries and devoutly religious friends can make me understand what it means to walk through this world as them. I may unintentionally use language or share experiences that offend and be told about it. Learn something new. Adjust my language in the future to make more room for all of us to breathe easier. My friends know I'm flawed and learning and not intentionally hurtful.

If I'm too quiet, or woo woo, or long winded, or short, or weepy, or non-religious, or white, or female, or honest about my perspective for you, I can leave, you can leave, or we can stay and imagine ourselves as something better together. I'm happy to flex and love to learn together, shift, change, adapt.

But after 40-ish years of apologizing for being me, I've finally stopped. I don't apologize for being me anymore. And I don't want you to either.

People in my world now are allowed to be themselves. All people. Even me.

Hint 46: If you feel unsafe, do something immediately.

For example, move, say something, ask for help, cry, yell, or leave.

Leaving and reflecting on what made you feel unsafe, then communicating about it somehow later in your own time, and then trying again, is a brilliant approach too. Don't let people tell you otherwise. When I think of people of action, this is who I think of. Likely because this is my preferred approach.

Another brilliant approach is leaving and never coming back, with no regrets.

Another brilliant approach is showing up and saying what makes you feel unsafe right from the beginning. I like this approach because it holds within it great potential for rest from carrying your burdens alone. The more people who know what makes you feel unsafe, the more burden is lifted from you and shifted onto the community, where burdens can feel lighter for everyone.

## Hint 47: When uncomfortable, reflect on why you think being uncomfortable is a bad thing.

If you feel annoyed, angry, stupid, frustrated, helpless, or lost, reflect on why you think these are bad things. Uncomfortable is not the same thing as unsafe. Discomfort causes us to reflect. Usually stays with us until we do.

Our space showed me that some people give the gift of making us feel wonderful and perfect, exactly as we are. They offer much-needed contentment and rest within a chaotic world. If I were a semi-nerdy gardener, I might say these people warm me like sunshine, ground me like soil, or envelop me like fog. Other people give the gift of making us feel annoyed, angry, stupid, frustrated, helpless, or lost. They might make us feel stunningly ill-equipped for the moment or shine a light on our biases or point out cracks in our personal safety nets of belief. These people offer much-needed discontent and growth within us. They don't allow us to stagnate. They are water, wind, clay, or rocks to little seedling me. Yes, I'm a gardening dork. We say weird things like this sometimes and refuse to change. Stick with me.

In a collaborative space where anyone can walk in, you have considerably more small chances from moment to moment to encounter discomfort. This also means a lot more tiny decision points where you must think about and decide what you're going to do about feeling discomfort.

In many cases, this means that working here is a little more uncomfortable, especially at the beginning, than a traditional day job because fewer choices about who gets in, who does what and how, who stays, and who doesn't have been made for you than at a day job. Here we make more of those choices for ourselves.

This also means, in many cases, that we get really good, relatively quickly, at moving with our own—and others—comfort and discomfort. Eventually we begin to automatically adjust without thinking about it—moving on instinct in the space. Learning to deeply trust our instincts. This can crack wide open where you are able to feel comfortable working in the future.

I write everywhere now: outside, sitting on the ground or at the end of a dock or walking the dog, in public spaces of all kinds, other collaborative spaces, on the ferry, in waiting rooms, in other people's homes, and even within online conversations. I can write with people present, write as part of groups, and create books in groups. Three years ago, the only place I could get any writing work done was in my home office with the door shut and alone.

I write on everything now, too. I always have things to write on: sand on the beach, driftwood and rocks, grocery receipts, paper notebooks, dirty car windows, post-its, phone, laptop, iPad, etc. And I don't just write anymore, thanks to the coworking space. I also paint, draw, sew, create collages out of cut up found illustrations (viva la modge podge!), and I've begun playing the piano again. The biggest creative gift—poetry—came after two years in the space, and then letting the space go to be alone for a while. I now turn discomfort into poetry. I now turn most things into poetry.

Creativity has gotten a whole lot easier for me thanks to the discomforts of working in a coworking space. Discomfort is my friend now too. Most days. Viva la disruptions!

## Hint 48: Don't work in the space.

Go to coffee with someone. Grab lunch with someone. Walk to the corner and grab a beer at Chucks.

Play in the space. Make cookies or whatever you make best. Get vacation ideas and parenting tips. Host a movie night. Or a root beer or honey tasting party. Test out jokes. Share hobbies and friend's art openings and recipes. Dream about a better neighborhood and your part in making it happen. You might find this "not-working" time is your favorite part. If playing at work guilts you out, remember that by playing you reveal things that you wouldn't otherwise reveal about yourself. As a result, you might be shown things about yourself that you hadn't considered—things that point you down a new way of thinking, or to a new idea, or in a new career direction, like our space did for me.

Play outside the space together. Hang out together elsewhere, or join in on neighborhood projects in-progress.

Consider running the space for an hour to give those running it every week a break. Some people running spaces are really good at asking for help. Others, like me, suck at it. All of us appreciate help now and then. From my perspective, anyone coworking often enough to be recognized as a vital community member is qualified to run an in-home space. Nobody runs an in-home space alone.

Letting Go of the Space

## Hint 49: Notice a shift in your energy.

In August 2013, I felt my energy for running the coworking space begin to lag. It began moving from something I couldn't wait to do to something I had to show up and do each week.

# Hint 50: Do nothing for a while.

If you can, slow down. Reflect on your decreasing energy. To the extent you can, do nothing for a while: the bigger the shift, the longer the nothing. Don't feel bad about this natural part of the cycle. This is a really good thing, even though it might not feel great at the beginning.

In August and September 2013, I went into a state that was almost, but not quite, depression. I didn't want to go anywhere. I didn't want to do anything. I reduced my writing workload to the extent I could. I stopped going out. I watched a lot of Sci Fi reruns. Ate more than my fair share of chocolate mousse. People thought I was crazy because we only get two reliably gorgeous months here—August and September—and everybody but me was outside basking in the sun and frequenting those lovely outdoor patios that we get to stare at from inside most of the year. I spent those two months freaking Daniel out, because I knew I wanted something significantly different, but I didn't know what yet. I tried to reassure him, but I wasn't exactly in a reassuring place. I was 98% sure I wasn't depressed. I was 98% sure that I wasn't unhappy with my life or my marriage or my career choices. But that 2% felt huge.

It wasn't depression, though. What I was doing was listening. Deep listening. It was like trees in winter: it looks like nothing is happening on the outside while a lot is happening on the inside. Such an important part of a healthy lifecycle. Why the frack didn't my culture teach me this?! But I digress...

As hard as it was to make a decision that might mean the end of the coworking space, I figured out that I was getting the urge to move. I first figured out that I wanted to move around a lot more—work in other people's spaces instead of running my own every week. I next figured out that after 21 years in the city, I was being pulled away from the city itself—feeling like it was time for a major shift to an empty, quiet place with wide-open horizons, similar to those I'd loved as a kid.

By the first week of October, I knew I wanted to move outside the city, hopefully near the ocean and beach: a place where Eva dog, Daniel, and I could live off leash.

Hint 51: Watch your energy skyrocket and shift back to your individual/ family needs.

Once I figured out what I really wanted, my energy began to skyrocket again. I tried to ease myself and Daniel into the idea of beach living outside the city by saying that it might take us two years to find the just-right place.

But he knew we'd be leaving very soon. He knew it before I did. He said that he suspected it'd be weeks, not years. This wasn't his first time witnessing an idea take hold of me or flexing to make room for the new.

Men are remarkably intuitive and flexible even though they too rarely acknowledge and talk about it.

They're also remarkably capable of relying on and supporting women's intuition as we move forward with certainty and without knowing all the whys. I think we too rarely thank them for it.

Thanks Daniel.

## Hint 52: This time notice that you trust your a-ha! moment implicitly.

So back in January 2012, I felt into my bones that turning our home into a community coworking space was a great idea (see Hint 4). I did it, yet I didn't fully trust that feeling back then. I was really nervous for at least the first 4 months I ran the space. Basically, I was nervous until I saw that we could do it.

By October 2013, I had changed. We had been profoundly changed by hosting community, including strangers, in our home every week, and by going out to work with other small organizations around the neighborhood together. When the a-ha moment showed up again, I trusted it considerably more this time—and so did Daniel—even though this time it was a much bigger life shift.

In early October, Daniel, Eva dog, and I began looking for homes outside the city. The cover of the book I'd just published (*A Travel Guide for Transitions*) had a pirate flag on it. Technically, a chicken pirate flag, but close enough. Two weeks into researching new communities and homes online and deciding which to visit, a quaint black house with white trim and green front door—flying a pirate flag—appeared before my eyes. It was 90 minutes from our Seattle house. In a small 100+-year-old, multi-generational beach neighborhood: an off-leash neighborhood.

I knew it the moment I saw it. Home. That house was home. The perfect place for a chicken pirate.

When we walked inside The Pirate House (what many Whidbey neighbors called it before we got here), I knew again. We were home. Daniel knew it too. The home had been calling to us. I still can't quite believe we were lucky enough to be in a position to hear our next home call to us. And to have it within us to move when she called. Or that we could afford to go. Or that we were brave enough to say goodbye to the home/space/neighborhood/city we loved. But we had all these things within us. Thanks in large part to the community surrounding our coworking space. A community that, by this time, stretched across the city.

Here you may begin to notice that my stories can be a bit woo woo. Don't be alarmed. Here in the Letting Go of the Space section, it's time to begin getting used to the woo. Some days, only woo will do.

This down-to-my-bones feeling was the exact feeling I had when I got the idea to start the coworking space in the first place. In less than two years of reimagining our private home as community space, I'd learned to deeply trust myself, our neighbors, our neighborhood, and our city. I knew the shift would be difficult at first. And I knew we could do it.

I didn't know how. I just knew that we could.

## Hint 53: Say "HELL Yes!" to community help. Witness magic.

By early November 2013, I was sitting at the big, round, 500-year table at the start of another coworking Wednesday worrying and wondering about how to tell everyone in the community that Daniel, Eva dog, and Joe, Bella, and Batman the cats would be leaving at the end of December. We were moving to Whidbey. To the Pirate House.

Nicole—a stranger to me—walked in the door. She introduced herself, and I quickly realized that she wasn't really a stranger. She was the partner of Alex, a friend who I'd met when she worked at Office Nomads. I love Alex. I trust everyone who runs (or has run) Office Nomads completely. I trusted Nicole, by association, too. She was a community member that instant. I have the words we said next, because I blogged about it at the time:

> Nicole sat down, sighed, and said sadly, "We've got to move! They found asbestos in our apartment's duct work!"
>
> I said, "What are you looking for?"
>
> She said, "A nice, shared place like this, in a walkable neighborhood, like this."
>
> I said, "Would you like our part of this place? I think we're moving."
>
> And she said, "Oh my God! Yes! And could we still do coworking out of here one day per week?"
>
> And I said, "Oh my God! HELL yes!"

I showed Nicole our part of the home—the second floor. And although she was trying to play it cool (I could see Alex telling her to do so in her head—after all, she didn't know if they could afford the space yet or if Alex would like it), she literally physically bounced up and down when I showed her around our part of the space. I had that exact same energy for the home when I'd walked through it 12 years earlier. My own sadness about leaving shifted, on the spot, into deep joy. I was so excited that Nicole loved the space deeply that today I strongly suspect that I was bouncing up and down a little bit at that point too. If trusted others moved in, I was pretty sure that Daniel and I could afford to keep the home for a while. We wouldn't have to sell it immediately. The space could continue serving as a community space.

Alex and Nicole came to see the space together, had a meal with us and met our house-mates, and fell in love with the people/space as we had. We moved out at the end of December. Two days later, they moved in.

We got to leave the CD knowing that our housemates, coworkers, and neighbors were all being left in kind, generous, and neighborly hands.

I got to watch as Collective Self Coworking began reinventing herself, in January 2014, with new high-energy humans and new cats in charge. The space, people, and neighbor-hood we dearly loved deserved nothing less.

# Hint 54: Let go with minimal sadness. You carry the space inside you now.

I spent most of 2014 watching Collective Self coworking reimagine herself from a distance. I was becoming a poet on Whidbey—turning the act of writing into full-on playing. Dealing with extended family meltdown too. I occasionally returned to cowork at Collective Self.

The first two months were hard for me, internally. I struggled with knowing how much help to offer Nicole. I wanted her to do things her own way. And I wanted to help her however I could. I didn't know where that line was between useful and pushy previous runner of the space—and it felt a bit awkward internally. It got easier as I could see that Nicole was fine, and I got busier with my own new life and work. Sometimes many months would pass between my visits to the space. Eventually I noticed that Nicole didn't seem to mind at all if I sent an occasional idea her way. I was, after all, a coworking space community member. Why would she mind? My ideas were just like any other community member's. I'm not the boss of her. I never was.

Things have changed in the space, and they continue changing: yet somehow what matters most to me has remained the same. It's funny. Back when I ran the space, I experienced almost everyone who showed up as a gift. It was like 99.9% percent of human beings were gifts, and every six months or so there'd be a brief visit from a jerk. Today, everyone who shows up to coworking—everyone—is a gift to me. Jerks don't scare me anymore. They're not whole separate people, like I once thought. The "jerk" is just a part of me. I made peace with the jerk inside me this year. And the weirdo. Don't even get me started on the dragon.

One of my favorite coworking days in 2014 was in the fall when a vanload of friends decided to bring coworking Wednesday out of the space in the Central District and onto Whidbey Island for the day—to our new house. We didn't get a lot of individual work done that day. Jane showed up with a kite, board games, and pie-making supplies. But we walked on the beach, played a cool Japanese board game, picked a ton of apples and crab apples, and made apple empanadas, apple pies, and mini apple pies in jars. Such a lovely day. Everyone departed with a bag full of apple pies. That night I realized that all my work, now, is actually play. So weird and awesome.

It's come clear that letting go when you feel it's time to let go—not hanging on too long out of fear—is an important part of deep loving and, from my perspective, of natural lifecycles. I think our in-home community space teaches this wordlessly, because the process itself is visible to core community members even when we don't talk about it. And when we do talk about it, it's relatively fast, fluid, natural, and just part of life. For example, this weekend Nicole and I went plant shopping Saturday morning. We talked about the fact that she just got a daytime-hours day job—and has to give up running coworking for a while—and the fact that five community members volunteered to help host in the space in her absence. Including—just 1 day/month if needed—me. But most of the time we talked about gardening, yard work, plants, cats, food, and art stuff. Because that's who we are too. And when we got home (to her home), we frosted cupcakes and then greeted Jane and Ryan who showed up to host their craft-centered birthday party in the space.

## Hint 55: Revel in being your more whole weird self—not the visible leader.

Being your more whole weird self is so much better than being the visible leader all the time. Why did my culture not teach me this? WTF culture? The coworking space is truly not mine to run now. Nothing is mine to fix or solve or mediate or plan. Nothing. I can let everything happen. I can listen to everyone. I love listening. I still get to practice becoming ok with whatever is—exactly as it is—in the moment.

When I'm moved to tears now—from wonder, empathy, sadness—I weep. When I'm hurt by something someone says, I allow myself to be visibly hurt. When I want to say something silly, weird, rude, or wrong, I don't stop myself. I say it. I watch what happens. When I have an idea for the space, I share it. I've decided to trust all humans—and the group—to be able to handle me exactly as I am. Often it seems far easier for them to trust me than for me to trust myself. So I define community as all the people who believe in me even when I don't believe in myself.

Now that I'm not the visible leader in the space, I get to play with a bunch of new ways of being that are opening to me now. For example, in February, in anticipation of visiting Seattle for one coworking Wednesday (when I also wanted input on this book), on Tuesday I flat out demanded that all my dear friends either a) stop by to see me during coworking or b) have a better reason for not being there than Madeleine, who was in Antarctica. I'm normally not demanding like this. This was new. I was playing with that part of me who fears being alone. I demanded their presence like I've always wanted to. I balled up my fists, jumped up and down like a small child, and demanded the attention of all my favorite people who I knew had at least a chance of being able to be there for a while on Wednesday. Fortunately, they could only see my demands via Facebook and Twitter, where I came across as slightly more grown up than I did in person. Then again, maybe not. My friends teased me, laughed, and all those who could show up for a little while, did. People are amazing.

It's difficult to explain how great it is to work in a community coworking space that you once ran but don't anymore. I just show up as Lori now. Like Beyoncé, Justin, Beck, Madonna, Prince, Cher, or Sinatra (that ought to cover the age range in our space)—I don't need job titles now. I don't even need two names. I love being just another writer and poet doing my own thing in the space now, not trying to run anything. Even better, I love that most people don't actually give a crap what I do for a living. They're just glad to see me and Eva dog (who also doesn't need titles). It's just. wow.

I've noticed that to show up more fully comfortable with yourself is a wordless gift to everyone present. I have my share of flaws, and I'm loved because of them now, not despite them. I've been loved by others here through my mistakes (some of them HUGE) and blind spots and tears and bad puns and discomfort and anger and poor word choices and bias and tired snappiness and long-windedness and over-focus on my individual work, and even through leaving and moving away. I've been loved as I've changed. I've been loved through refusing to change what I love most about myself: being a wondering, wending, writing wanderer with an almost unshakable faith in awe, gratitude, play, and the deep magic locked within us. I will never stop being long-winded about things that deeply matter to me. Once it was because I couldn't help myself. Now it's because I won't help myself. My self is fine. She's a poet and a flash non-fiction author now. The girl's got this.

Core community members—people who experience themselves as important to the community—get to witness that the love here lasts, no matter where we go or what we do. We get to witness that it's ok to be exactly who we really are—everything we perceive as good and bad about ourselves. The community demonstrates that it is strong enough to hold all parts of us. As the community demonstrates it, we believe it, become capable of making peace with even more parts of ourselves, and then, with more parts of others.

At least that's how it keeps working for me.

## Hint 56: Don't let go of the space.

The sky's the limit on new things to do with community space once private space has been reimagined as community space.

Two years in, Daniel and I let go of living in our home and I let go of running the co-working space within it. Nicole took over, and I left for months on end. But the space lives inside me. I didn't actually let go. It's now been 15 months since I left, and I still pop in now and then to create, work, help, reconnect, and play.

This week, it's Nicole's turn to let go of running the space as she takes on a new day-time-hours day job. Viva la health benefits! But she's not exactly letting go either. She and I went plant shopping for the yard on Saturday, and then we went to Jane and Ryan's Saturday crafternoon birthday party, which they decided to host in the Collective Self coworking space, aka Nicole's house, aka, our house.

And five community members immediately volunteered to take over hosting coworking in Nicole's absence, so the space itself isn't quite done yet apparently, either. Even with Nicole shifting roles.

I'm sure Nicole's worrying about leaving a bit, like I did. But she'll soon see that it's really fun to be involved in watching the space reimagine itself. What will it become next? A place of shared space-running responsibilities? Coworking days or times reimagined? The space reimagined as a different kind of community space entirely—artist work space, board-game-playing space, community dinner space, writer's grotto, a community re-source center for neighborhood parking strip gardeners? Asking other neighbors to open their homes as community spaces? I don't see a limit.

I strongly suspect both Nicole and I will be curious enough, and so around enough but not too much, to help with the transition.

Hint 57: If handing off the space to someone else, tell them three things about running the space, then stop.

When I handed off the space to Nicole 15 months ago, she got two long email messages from me about running the space. Too much, I suspect. When Elyse took over this month, I offered no advice at all until asked. Elyse received three ideas from me followed by a list of neighbors and local organizations she could introduce herself to because she specifically asked for neighbor contacts.

The idea is to not bog down the next generations with your ideas and preferences. Offer just enough to give them confidence that they've got this then shut the hell up. So three things up front, then stop. If they need more, let them ask. Our Facebook page contains lots of space history and photos. People are wise. If they want to continue traditions they will. If they don't, they won't. No matter what we say.

Elyse:

> I'm wondering if there was a primer or anything you shared with Nicole when you passed off coworking to her. Obviously, I can just ask her as well, but I wanted to see if you had any vision or guidelines that you'd like to see stay consistent with Collective Self. What's been your policy on keeping coffee/tea here? Is that an expense I will take over as a labor of love to share with coworkers?

> Also, I've been thinking I might go knock on some neighbor's doors soon just to introduce myself. I realize I spend the first few months here just kind of getting into a new rhythm. Now that I'm settled, I'd love to know who some more of the neighbors are! Anyone in particular you think I should know / reach out to?

Lori:

> What matters most to me about the space during coworking is that those who show up feel welcome and honored as neighbors. Even if our space isn't the right space for them: they feel listened to, appreciated, and honored enough as neighbors that they might recommend our space to others. But don't worry about that. I wouldn't have chosen you to live in the house and be a neighbor to our neighbors, and you wouldn't be interested in hosting coworking, if you weren't naturally already good at that.

> I think it's more important for you to be aware of what matters most to you about coworking and that you stay true to that. Just one thing, whatever it is.

> Re tea and coffee, what you'll find about hosting a regular free space is that you're automatically part of the gift economy. People show up generous and bring gifts of tea, coffee, and many other things. I always just told people to bring what they wanted if they wanted something specific. When we ran low, and people asked what they could do to help, I'd tell them tea/coffee/toilet paper. :) I did occasionally supplement the tea with a kind I liked. You could also put an empty jar by the tea with a "tea fund" sign on it. I never tried that. I prefer direct useful gifts over cash.

> All these awesome neighbors…

Who's That Playing in the Space Between?

## Hint 58: Embracing the stranger in yourself.

I am still a stranger. I think a little strangerhood is good for us. Keeps us moving and learning. These days, for me it seems, the stranger the better.

The difference today is that now I shift often between telling the story and being a character in it. I get to be an adventurer, a stranger, an artist, and a storyteller. Old me was a character in somebody else's story: one who tended to feel doomed to spend months and years trapped in a state of chronic strangerhood—the state of feeling like a visitor on my own planet, in my own country, in my own city, in my own neighborhood, and even in my own body.

The new me is something else. Shifting. Moving. Quirky. Powerful. Artist. Weird. Creative. Adventurer. Dragon. That Lori. She's quite a character.

I see in-home neighborhood coworking spaces (and other types of regular in-home community spaces) and other community-focused coworking spaces helping us embrace the stranger in ourselves—in one way or another—for those of us who stay connected to these spaces and to each other.

Everyone who opens that door and steps through it is signing on to tell their own story. And to become part of a new story in which strangers are cool too.

The space teaches that strangers are ok—we make them so ourselves—and that we are ok even when we ourselves show up as strangers. It reminds us we are adventurers. Risk takers. Chicken pirates even.

As we embrace these parts of ourselves, the space reimagines us as friends, coworkers, artists, collaborators, neighbors, chefs, gardeners, crafters, makers, parents, friendship creators, community re-creators, and city re-inventors. We fly our weirdo flags visibly and proudly. Across one boundary after another as we recognize others—strangers—just doing the same.

The space continues to reimagine my fears of the stranger, the dangerous, the scary, and the monsters. I don't even have to be there in person anymore for this to be true. It's quite convenient.

Most days strangers and dangers are interesting new characters and plot twists in the story I'm living and writing. When I'm drowning, I mermaid. When I'm shattering, I dragon. When you are, I hug you, listen, and maybe make you tea and cookies. Or I dragon with you. Why not? I can.

Or you can just work here.
That's fine too.

Hint 59: Keeping a kind stranger generator in your basement. In case of emergency.

that one time
there was a time
a time
I couldn't control
which strangers were kind and
which weren't

Now's not that time.

Behold the kind stranger generator!
a living, breathing, walking game, my friends
(my bitches, some might say)
love you guys

here
right here
in my presence
just in this little space

here

most people
all dogs and cats
sense the choice
opt to play

we play
spontaneously
intuitively
indubitably or
out bubitably
play our asses off
actually

wait, what?

where was it? where is it?
the moment it happens

the moment this place
taught me good
butt good
that I always have a choice

Damn, girl.
smooth

Hint 60: Bowing in deep gratitude for this life.

Today I get tears in my eyes every time I witness our home and work space fill with community. Every time I think about watching the space move on so fluidly into the hands of amazing others. Every time I realize that the space and place surfaced the poet and the artist in me. Brought back the old me. The real me. The girl sitting in the sand writing poetry and painting rocks.

What a gift this place is. What a gift this life is.

Words fail.

Hint -11,385.1a: Embracing the quirky weirdo in yourself.

## Hint 62: Playing together to remember all life as a gift we receive.

Instead of struggling alone for what I think I need, here in the space between we play together regularly—which makes what I need visible and allows the community to gift what we really need to us. Teaches us about receiving…

Friends and renters as gifts. We still own the home where the official Collective Self coworking space lives. But we moved away 15 months ago. Today, three of the four humans living there—Alex, Nicole, and Elyse—plus cats Teo and Spice, are there thanks to Susan, our mutual friend at Office Nomads. All these lovely people just showed up on our doorstep. Gifts. The fourth human, Isaac (also lovely), is there thanks to our mutual friend, neighbor-turned-coworker-turned-friend-turned-crafting-guru-turned-creative-collaborator Tabitha. More gifts.

Home improvement as gifts. One summer coworkers-and-neighbors-turned-friends Tabitha and Jon needed a place to stay while they sold their home and looked for a new one. They moved in to our backyard cottage and Tabitha fixed up the cottage—painting every wall, door, and piece of trim. She cleaned places I was scared to even look—like behind the ancient stove. She restored old painted door knobs and wall-heater covers—something I'd never have had the patience to do. She even put leftover paint in little plastic tubs, and labeled them: wow. Gifts.

Creative work partners as gifts. Tabitha and I cowork outside the physical space now—collaborating on books and art projects and gardening and helping ourselves make peace with our strange-even-to-ourselves nature as artists. She works from her house. I work from mine. We work together. She gifts presence, illustrations, crafting and home improvement and marketing skills, technical expertise, and hosting game nights. I've gifted visits to the beach, curating a Collective Self art show at Office Nomads, space to host crafting workshops, found-object art supplies, and money. Bas and I gifted creation of our three books to ourselves. We each just paid for bits on our ends, working for the joy of being together. These friends are family now. They're helping me learn how to make a living as an author. Gifts.

Significant others as gifts. When I ran coworking, Daniel had a day job and couldn't join us on Wednesdays. But the magic of the space wasn't lost on him. Today D and I cowork one or two days/week together in local coffee shops and bookstores. Another gift beyond measure from my time running the space: a husband who dropped his day job to just three 10-hour days/week to spend more time with me, photography and teaching photography (his true passions), and our little artist business. He helps non-tech-Lori-brain figure out how to self-publish books too. Gifts.

New work processes and books as gifts. A month ago, I showed up to work at Collective Self for the day and Nicole mentioned that she was in her second year running the space. I realized that February was the third anniversary of the space itself opening. The idea for this book came from our time together that day. This is a book I wish I'd been able to gift to Nicole a year ago, but I'm not exactly a fast learner. Fortunately, she's tough—an artist—and does fine on her own. The opportunity to create a flash-non-fiction book in a month was a gift the space gave to me. I've never tried flash non-fiction: it's got me totally rethinking my book creation process. Nothing is expected in return, of course. That wouldn't be a gift. But I can't wait to hand Nicole, Forrest, Elyse, and others, copies of this book, as a gift. Yay!

# Hint 63: Happening upon beauty and fun everywhere.

As someone who once ran the coworking the space, I know there's housework involved and that those running the space have a lot going on in their lives. Sometimes when I visit coworking now, I do little things I know aren't particularly fun for Nicole—for the pure fun of it.

For example, it's so much fun to take out the trash, clean the kitchen sink, wipe down the counters, and clean the bathroom. I love gifting service to the community!

I know sometimes supplies run low when a lot of people work in your house, so I've snuck in and gifted pretty hand soap, and spare hand towels, and even toilet paper to the bathroom. I gift homegrown tea to and home canned foods to Nicole/the housemates/ the kitchen. I gift rocks from the Whidbey beach to coworkers. I gifted the ridiculously awesome, Chris-discovered, feather-thing-on-a-fishing-lure-on-a-stick cat toy to Spice and Teo. These are all deep fun things for me now, since I'm only around once a month. I love gifting practical little things to others.

There was a time, many years ago, when these things were innately fun for me. Then somewhere along the way they became not fun. Chores. Today, they're deep fun. Deep fun lands me in the presence of deep beauty again and again. I love this, being a big fan of awe and all. I see Letting Go of the Space as crucial to my new-found ability to experience deep fun and deep beauty almost everywhere I go now.

When I say deep (which I maybe should have explained back in Hint 3, but there it wouldn't have been much fun), I mean that I experience them more as gifts given to me generously by the whole place than as things that I somehow made happen myself. If you want to hear more about deep, especially deep fun, ask my friend Bernie. He's been swimming in the deep since before I was born. I only dog paddle.

Part of dog paddling in the deep involves listening carefully, wordlessly, to hear that my fun is fun for Nicole too. It is her house now, after all: mine only in title. If my fun isn't fun for her too, I'm just a creepy landlord. As near as I can tell, my cleaning up after coworking, or adding a roll or two of toilet paper now and then, is fun for her too.

Hint 64: Watching life for deep words, community stories, and little reminders.

I like encountering words, stories, music, poetry, art, and little reminders that highlight what matters most within a community without explicitly saying what matters most. Deep words prefer being part of the mystery. They think so highly of people—all people—that they feel compelled to leave clues, not answers. I asked. This is why they show up fully in stories, music, and poetry. Why almost nobody likes reading manuals and textbooks. We can sense the words are just furious about being dumped in such dead boring places. It's the words that were lived that live on within us.

Thirteen years ago, our next-door neighbor Charlie told us the story of sitting on his front porch after he retired, day after day, year after year, to protect both the neighborhood trees that he planted and the kids who'd been damaging them. Deep words. Gifts. When Charlie died, we wept. And we keep looking out for his trees and neighbors. We keep passing on his stories.

Ask me how many words I remember from my 8+ years at Microsoft. The answer is 25. I remember a friend's words from my last day there. Kim was my boss' boss who I had the great fortune to work with closely on a multi-year pet project of ours as more like peers, which was a treat considering he was older and wiser and cool, and I was quite the naïve and nerdy kid. We sat side by side on the floor among many others and many boxes piled in his new office (the team had just moved) sharing a drink during a snowstorm that had rapidly shut down the city. A large group of strangers had just come in to warm up after their bus got stuck in the snow. Nobody could go home immediately, so employees broke out food and drinks of all kinds and slowed down into gracious hosts. The place was feeling festive. So I wasn't at all prepared for Kim saying this:

> You've been our ethical compass. I'm thinking of getting the team WWLD? bumper stickers so we remember to keep asking ourselves "What Would Lori Do?"

Deep words. I wept. That was 8 years ago. Kim just left Seattle for a new job in New York City last week. When I heard the news, my heart broke. He consoled us by letting us know he'd be back one day. Thank God. Washington State isn't the same without him. Today I know Kim as a musician: one of the best harmonica players and band leaders in the country, IMO. Not a half bad singer, either. ;-) And dead sexy on stage. He also surfs organizational politics like a jazz musician riffing with friends. When I encounter politicking humans that I don't think I can handle, I still think "What would Kim do?"

This week, after I posted a poem to the Collective Self Facebook page, Nicole sent me this gift:

> Dear Lori, After reading the poem today, I wanted to thank you for the opportunity to live in your home and to be entrusted to run Collective Self. Both have meant so much to me. Living in your home has provided me with a safe and beautiful place to help me heal more quickly from my back injury. The studio room has provided me with a dedicated space to meet my artistic side again. The house has provided me with wonderful roommates that have provided support and friendship. Collective Self has provided me with another beautiful community in my life. Your friendship and guidance with Collective Self has provided me with calm and confidence. And these are just a few of the ways living here have impacted my life and helped me grow and thrive. Thank you, thank you, thank you. With deep gratitude, Nicole

Yeah, no spoilers. I wept again. Deep words. She even used the word deep! Wah! I'm so proud of her.

We humans don't need to be told what matters most. We live it. We feel it physically from within—in laughter, tears, a lump in the throat, a knot in the stomach, goose bumps, in the hair on the back of our neck standing up, and in bouncing up and down with excitement.

According to deep words, which I listen to regularly now, we human folk just need little reminders along the way that we're already part of what matters most. Little reminders along the way of who we really are and what we're really capable of. Little reminders of our connection to the larger story we're all part of. Reminders that we are the creators of our stories and the created.

Stories show up to do that for us, just like neighbors and friends.

## Hint 65: Experiencing connections within and across stories

Living them together makes them easier to notice…

First story: The book begins with my own brief history of falling in love with the Central District.

Second story: The story of a coworking space. The lifecycle of an in-home coworking space tells its own story. The space watches as we imagine, run, work in, let go, and play within her walls. Found-object art and visual mementos from our 3+ years together are included on the book's covers and at the end of the book for the fun of it.

Third story: The reader's story. Each section of this book contains a handful of short-ish hints from our space for people imagining and living a similar story elsewhere. Read the hints that matter most to you depending on where you are in your own story.

Fourth story: The story of community. Stories from Collective Self Coworking and the Seattle Collaborative Space Alliance are woven throughout the book. We're also threads in a larger story of community.

Fifth story: The story of neighborhood. Stories from the Central District are woven throughout the book. We are threads in her larger story too.

Sixth story: The story of city and region. Stories from Seattle and the region are here too, for those who listen closely. We are threads in her larger story.

Seventh story: This book ends with my own brief-ish story about how the region, city, neighborhood, and community coworking space are reimagining me today.

Eighth story: This book is the fifth book in what I just figured out are a lived-adventure series. The author, the cover illustrators, and many of the other characters in this book are off living and adventuring in our other books as well. The final pages of this book contain pointers to our other lived-adventure series books.

## Hint 66: Living beyond conventional (for you) ideas, expectations, and roles.

Back when I ran the coworking space, I used to explain all my actions and beliefs out loud all the time. That's what I did to reveal/create/build community then. A lovely way to do things. And. I often over-shared. Eyes would glaze. Go search on the word "coworking" in the Collective Self blog and read entries from 2012 if you don't believe me. Or ask anyone who knows me. Also, language itself is a barrier. The words you choose to communicate with one person won't work for another, no matter who you are. This is a hard reality for most storytellers and writers to face.

Eventually I decided to trust the community, and myself, fully, which led me to move 90 minutes away and leave the space for months on end, trusting others to carry on without me. I gifted my absence. Today I can't over-share in person, I'm not at coworking often enough. When I am there, I listen way more than speak. I'm a natural learner in person, not a teacher. It took physically moving to an island to quell my non-stop yammering about coworking, community, and self-organizing groups. I can still overshare in a book, of course, and my techniques are shifting so I don't as often. Then again, why deprive people of the deep joys to be found in skimming? Or in slowing down, going deeper, when they want to? Wending in a book is more fun. We do so on our own terms.

After we moved away from our CD home, as I got closer to the community in 2014—listening more closely when I visited because I was there less—during coworking other people's words began to matter more and more to me, yet fewer words seemed necessary from me. It was weird and awesome.

Listening more, paired with my new need to say less, led me to writing poetry: far fewer words, but wow, do those words count. I'd never have had the courage to recognize myself as a poet or ever call myself a poet. But by April 2014, two of my new neighbors on Whidbey showed up to introduce themselves—having read my blog—and they called me a poet. The title was a gift from strangers and neighbors. I was stunned. I had no idea I was a poet. As a result of their gift, I published my first book of poetry in December 2014. My next one I suspect will be out by October 2015. I'm writing a 5-year series for new poets demonstrating that being a poet is more about chaos/routine/recognizing self than about individual talent or skill. Crazy. Who gets to be a poet? Nobody gets to be this lucky. I come from a mostly blue collar and redneck family. What the hell is happening with me? I don't understand how what I am now is even possible for me. This has been true for a few years now. I don't fully understand the magic of community. Today I don't feel the need to understand. I have daily practices in place that pull new friends toward me and put me in the way of witnessing daily magic. I feel deep power in what we've done and are doing now. Feel remarkably connected to my home planet. That's plenty.

By late 2014, being a poet helped me recognize myself as an improv comedy troupe member—go Team Jinda!— surrounding my parents with love and levity as we move into year 9 living with mom's Alzheimer's disease. My dragon. We craft deep discomfort and chaos into deep joy together now. When we fail—as we did when my extended family shattered this year—we weep and laugh together. My personal secret weapon is watching ridiculous reruns (a la Gilmore Girls, Scrubs, or Love Boat) to regroup within and after a shatter. We are funny, formidable, and fierce together. Dragons with a penchant for stand-up comedy. I'm writing a book now for other long-term care partner improv troupes like ours.

As 2015 began, I re-committed to working at Collective Self coworking one day/month. As a coworker today, I aspire to listen 99% of the time, say relatively little in person, and enjoy watching new members figure things out for themselves. The coworking community has created space within me to be able to do this. Has gifted me a life/career of playing/ working with friends, listening, creating, and writing—all my favorite things. You're welcome to tell me that this is unbelievable. I completely agree.

# Hint 67: Letting go of planning.

Today I like the idea of planning as a last resort if no amount of playing together works.

Guess how much planning I do? Less than an hour a week now. Many weeks, none at all.

Don't ask me how or why this works. I don't understand it myself and at this point I don't really want to. It's magic. Try to break it down and you'll get a bunch of parts, and robots trying to put them back together, not magic. Magic is found in the whole. In the mystery.

I do know that the coworking space—and all the friends I've made through it, and because of it—regularly tip me on my ear (metaphorically), shake me up, and pour bad ideas out of my head faster than my individual self can shovel new ones into it.

I know that I once was a list maker extraordinaire (my lists had sub lists), a borderline neat freak and control freak (some would say I was on the freak side of those borders), and a researcher. As a researcher, I can say that there's been overwhelming evidence in my life over the past 10 years that I don't need to run things as an individual anymore that it is purely practical, based on solid science, to give it up. I needed a ridiculous amount of proof, but I'm finally convinced that community playing and small group playing are the bigger buckets that a little planning now and then on my part floats around in.

I no longer feel like it's my business to plan my life. I experience that as the business of my community now. I commit myself to being present to the best of my ability and to showing up each day for the work, the play, and the people I love. That's plenty.

Besides, somehow Daniel learned to appreciate lists over the past few years, so if we really need a list now, he makes one.

## Hint 68: Shattering.

I shattered this year as my family shattered.

My mother has Alzheimer's disease. My father's been caregiving for 9 years and his own health and well-being have taken a hit. My sister and I are care partners for both of them now. My extended family has been in a court battle over my grandparents' estate for a year and a half. Too many of my once-close family can't stand each other now. So much hate now. Some days I choke on it.

Many in my family won't speak to each other at all now. Some quietly drifted away. Some cut ties with us because they can't handle our pain on top of their own. One I cut ties with because after a year of inflexible rage I realized that I was actually talking to a wall not a person, and so was she. I've been told my poetry is experienced by some as bashing the family and that my immediate family is no longer experienced as part of the larger family. Some are certain that their ties are broken forever. Some cry for weeks on end. Those not speaking to each other tend to make wild assumptions about the motives and stories being told by the other side. There are apparently "sides" now and a lot of us don't recognize that taking sides and creating sides are the same thing. Some of the people who spent decades teaching me to love tried--and failed--to teach me to hate. Game changer! It's bizarre. They rage at each other. Rage to anyone who'll listen, actually. Sometimes they appear to enjoy imagining and saying the worst. Many feel torn in half. Betrayed. I know I do.

If you want to remain in the Keep Calm and Carry On world forever, by all means, don't come here. Don't enter the space between.

Here we rage. We fail. We scream. We yell. We weep. We make huge, unforgiveable mistakes. We fight. We flee. We watch our hands become axes as we cut ties with those we love/hate/must move away from to survive. Wonder if those sharp axes will ever be reimagined into poet's hands again.

Here we shatter.

We shatter.

From Keep Calm and Carry On Land, we may appear crazy. Out of control. Scary. Broken. Dangerous.

Oh but we aren't. We are living a different kind of life is all: a wilder, wider, always-moving-now life.

One life is a pond. It is calm and serene on the surface. Its danger is stagnation and limited self-reflection pointing only at the sky. In humans this can show up as stability. Without shatter, though, it can also show up as rigidity, self-righteousness, losing touch with beyond-self reality, and choking on a festering stew of your own judgments and imagined monsters. I don't have to imagine this. I live it.

Life within the shatter is more like a river. Its danger is flooding and overwhelm. In humans, this can show up as flexibility, empathy, and exploring the nature of things far beyond the self/pond. Without some stability, though, it can also show up as being so far out of control that you visibly cause harm to yourself and anyone in your path. I don't have to imagine this life either. I live with shatter every day now.

Shattering is not easy. The shattering of my mom's memory is heartbreaking some days: wonder-filled and awe-inspiring and beyond amazing other days. This past year, the shattering of my entire family was so heartbreaking it felt like I was going to die. In case you're wondering, I didn't.

I became a family elder. Cut ties with some relatives (and some cut ties with me) to have more energy for supporting my parents, sister, aunt, cousins, husband, and self.

I became sillier. I binge watched all 153 episodes of Gilmore Girls on Netflix to mend my broken heart. A show that I'd never watched before and written off in passing as ridiculous, harmful, sexist, girly pop-culture brainless fluff. (Gosh, I'm not judgmental at all, am I?). The show mended a little girl's broken heart. This little girl, age 44. My sister and I then reimagined ourselves as an improv comedy caregiving troupe: Team Jinda.

I became a dragon. I spoke my truth in person, in poetry, and in essays and drew the wrath of extended family, who screamed "You know that's not true!" at me for sharing my perspective. It worked. Those previously inclined to rage at my exhausted father and my pregnant sister turned their eyes and their rage on me. Or tried to anyway. It's remarkably hard to fuck with a dragon. Especially a poet dragon who works part time as part of an improv comedy troupe. I am a person now comfortable in the presence of pure rage. Yours and mine.

Those who appear crazy, out of control, dangerous, scary, or broken don't scare me as much now. Those who rage, scream, fail, yell, weep, fight, flee, or make unforgiveable mistakes don't scare me either.

That's just my people.

People who shattered. Survived. And got remarkably fluid, powerful, and silly in the process.

We move together like a river.

We mix metaphors like fancy cocktails with little umbrellas.

Here within the shatter, the sign in the window always glows Open. Wide open, actually. Except for the brief moments it glows Get The Fuck Out and Let's Try Again Next Year.

## Hint 69: Taking my name and titles off my business cards and losing them entirely.

We are so much more than what we've been settling for.

If you are a stranger and we meet somewhere that I would have traditionally given you my business card, today you will receive a community gift from me instead: a hug, a book, a bookmark, a tip or idea, and/or a jar of home canned goods (pickles, jam, tomatoes, cherries, or crab apple liqueur usually).

An embrace—a hug—means we already recognize and like each other from earlier in the story. It means I love you and I missed you.

A tip or idea means I'm listening to you and think maybe this will help you.

A book means I trust you, I'm listening deeply, and I know this will help you.

I give bookmarks to strangers as a game. I hand them to people as if they're business cards. But they don't have my name or my titles on them: just a beloved image from one of my books, a thank you for supporting local authors and bookstores, and a picture of a poetry-spreading dragon-powered dirigible that Tabitha drew for me for the fun of it when I mentioned that the only way book marketing would ever be fun was if a dragon-powered poetry-spreading dirigible showed up to help me. That Tabitha. Some people like this mystery, play, and become friends and community members as a result. Others don't. Dragons are so efficient.

A jar of home canned goods means that you're a physically present neighbor and community member who I either adore (like family) or can't stand (like family). Either way, you are a person I want to spend more time with. I write my email address on the jars in case you want to reconnect later to talk home canning, gardening, or backyard bartering, want to swap recipes, discuss the meaning of life, or anything really.

I had to give up having business cards with my name and titles on them this year. It was bittersweet to see them go. I can't put words into dead-boring places anymore—I love them too much now. Also, titles can't contain me anymore. Which I mostly experience as a good thing, yet printing current-to-the-me-of-the-moment business cards became an effort in futility and wasting paper. So I had to let them go. Fortunately, Tabitha's dragon burned them to ashes. So going back to them isn't even an option.

# Hint 70: Moving like the wind.

On February 4, 2015, my regular practice of deep listening when present at Collective Self coworking allowed me to be the person who heard what would be needed next.

I decided to create this flash non-fiction book for the community, in 4 weeks, for the pure fun of it. Although I've never attempted flash non-fiction before, I committed to stop writing the book by March 5th and publishing it, in whatever form it was in, by mid-March. I asked for community input during that brief 4-week window, and in person once, on Feb 18th, during a coworking Wednesday.

We decided to gift this book to community members mentioned in the book by name. If you read about yourself, stop by the house and pick up your free copy in 2015, starting in April.

The last week of February, Nicole got a new daytime-hours day job. So on March 2nd, she announced that she will be unable to host coworking like she's been doing the past 14 months. Leaving a Nicole-shaped hole in our coworking space.

In the 24 hours that followed, five community members (that I know of)—Elyse, Forrest, Jane, brand-new community member Katja, and I—volunteered to help host coworking. Only Elyse lives in the house: all the rest of us are neighbors and friends. This is an amazing testament to Nicole and how well she ran the space. Bravo!

Ironically, I'm the one hosting Coworking Thursday on April 9th. The week the paperback version of this book becomes available.

Do I have the book for us! ;-)

## Hint 71: Falling deeply in love with space and place and people.

Turning our home into a community space supported me in falling more deeply in love with both our space—the home and the coworking space in it—and the place that holds them—the Central District neighborhood. Falling more deeply in love with the people here, in particular, and with people in general.

I can't believe that I forgot I had it in me to deeply love a place. Growing up in South Dakota, I loved my neighborhood as a kid and, in the summer, at our family's little lake cabin (more shack back then), I loved sitting at lake's edge, reflecting and writing. I loved becoming place. Then again, my people—explorers, pioneers, dreamers, wanderers, land owners, nomadic workers, the too-busy, landlords, and individuals who try to rush the process of influencing others—maybe tend to forget this more than others.

The CD grounded me. She reminded me of the value and importance of place.

The black community in the neighborhood—both long-time, seen-it-all residents and also new immigrants from mostly eastern African countries—are where most of the thanks for this belong. Your communities so clearly deeply understand the grounding value of place. Many others in the city just don't get this to the depth that you get it. They flat out forget that we're standing on, held by, mother earth, mother city, mother neighborhood.

It might be too late for the CD—more than half the black community has been pushed out already as new money has flooded into the city over the past 20 years. Or maybe not. If there is one community that has even an outside chance of saving rapidly growing Seattle from gentrification—from selling her soul block by block to the highest bidder who then pushes out everything that made her her to begin with—it will be the black community and those who stand with her. In the city, where the money-hungry come, we stand together as neighbors and reimagine our neighborhoods together, or we stare helplessly from our windows as huge out-of-neighborhood development companies reimagine them for us—too often into soulless, shiny bastions of sameness, blindness, and greed.

We moved to Whidbey last year. A new self to love, a new place to love. My deep love of the CD still sits at the dead center of me. That love has broadened to the whole of Seattle now: a city that received a clueless, broke, scared, relatively skill-free 22-year-old wanderer and in 20 years reimagined her as a good neighbor, decent gardener, community coworking space founder, and author. The city knocked away what didn't serve us and lifted up the me that matters most to me: the wanderer and the dreamer. Thank you Seattle.

I loved the house, the community space within it, and the neighborhood when I lived there and ran the space. I love them even more today. Today the city itself is sacred ground to me. When I return, I listen more closely and walk more softly and offer gratitude and gifts of thanks in my wake. I live in awe at what her people are doing. I believe in them. I love you. All of you. What a gift you are.

# Hint 72: Recognizing the space between as home, too.

Daniel and I moved away from the Central District and Collective Self Coworking 15 months ago. At the time, even though it felt like it was the right move for us, we didn't know why. To leave the home, the coworking space, and the neighborhood we loved was heartbreaking. It felt like we were letting go of them entirely. And we did let go, for a little while. But they've all come back to us.

As it turns out, I really needed a different place—quiet and wide-open horizon space like I had as a kid—to deal with my own extended family shattering this year, my growing involvement as a care partner for my parents, my exploration of myself as poet and soon-to-be new aunt. The CD knew that. She nudged me to go. Whidbey knew that too. She called me to her. Yes, I listen to neighborhoods and oceans now. That's me now. I've learned to trust our instincts and listen to whole places: water, trees, wind, sky, earth, movement, noise, stillness, silence, people, dogs, cats, bugs, birds, deer, and squirrels.

Somehow letting go made my connections to the space and place stronger than ever. Here in the emptiness of our new home, I've come to see that there is a way of living/working/playing that connects you so deeply to a place that you never fully let go. Collective Self Coworking is part of that way for me.

Life on earth isn't as hard as I once imagined it to be. I say that having dealt with my family shattering this year, my mom's Alzheimer's and dad's accompanying decline for 9 years, and conscious of the significant privileges and blindnesses that attend being a light-skinned, straight, relatively financially well-off American in 2015. What I mean is that it's really not ALL on humans to fix everything, like I used to imagine it was. Community spaces help us. Closer neighbors help, whole neighborhoods help, trees and plants of all sorts help, wildlife helps, safe walkways and streets help, bicycles help, bodies of water help, travel helps, stillness helps, night skies help, sunshine and snow and rain and fog help, children help, playful adults help, shifting weather and water helps, digging in the dirt or sand helps, walking helps, vegetables and fruits help, music helps, whole cities, and even islands, help. Silence helps some days. Noise helps other days. Here in the space between we become present for all this, see all this, receive help from everywhere.

There are places so amazing that they become part of you and you never fully let them go, no matter where you go. South Dakota, the Central District neighborhood, the city of Seattle, and Whidbey are part of me now. Yes, and…

I have another new home. I live and work in the spaces between. The space between day job and home life. The space between people. The space between words. The space between streets, between neighborhoods. The space between urban and rural. The space between buildings. Between land and water. Between sea and sky. Between this me and that me. I live in the space between imagining things, running things, working on things, and letting things go. Here I become ok with encountering beauty—vast stretches of it and little pockets of it—everywhere I go. Here I get lost and learn to trust my instincts and those of strangers. I decide to dance with chaos. I shatter. I craft art from the raw materials of experience, so all experience is art now. Here I make peace with others never seeing exactly what I see.

The space between is beyond messy. And its home now, too. Took me decades of cleaning before company came to visit, and three years of knocking that shit off, to realize that messy is a deeper welcome.

## Hint 73: Accepting the child's gift: deep imagination.

In the CD, there is deep beauty everywhere just waiting to be discovered. Amazing schools and churches. Kick-ass libraries and librarians. Kind and quirky neighbors. Parks and artwork and annual parades and events left as neighbor legacies. Amazing food. Lovely impromptu markets. Beautiful gardens and passionate gardeners. Amazing hair salons and neighborhood pubs where shop owners aren't just shop owners but community gurus and guides and service providers without limit. Amazing residents long accustomed to devoting their lives to fights that appear un-winnable in their lifetimes. People who don't shy away from sharing their perspective. Neighbors banding together across wide differences to make the neighborhood better. Schools where teachers, students, and parents protest side by side. Explorers of history and meaning. Jazz festivals and two-mile-long hopscotch paths.

You can't throw a rock here without hitting an artist of some sort: a musician, a sculptor, a painter, a dancer, a filmmaker, a crafter, an illustrator, a parent, a game designer, a community play guru, or a writer, for example. So many choose to dance with chaos here. The place is still covered with small- and micro-organization creators/business owners/farmers who opt to live/play/work with their neighbors instead of bowling them over. Dozens of little organizations and businesses and hundreds of individuals work together on Hopscotch CD: people with time and energy to physically show up to work/help/party/celebrate/clean up as neighbors.

I miss everything about her when I'm away. In this neighborhood, you can't blindly ignore our society shattering like many people elsewhere can. Gunfire in a city's streets is loud and visible shatter. We hear it, look at it, live with it, and co-imagine ways to change.

I find deep beauty on Whidbey as I wander here now too. Starkly different and yet remarkably similar.

Stumbling on deep beauty tends to generate feelings of deep hope. Tends to pop us into imagining something new. Tends to remind us that the space between is everywhere. It's all hope and magic up in here. Its pirates and mermaids and dragons and invention and imagination 24 x 8. In the space between, we re-accept play. We accept the deep work of being undone and remade that is always present in play.

In imaging a community space, running the space, working in the space, and letting go of that space, we accept the grownup tasks of being creators and storytellers ourselves.

Here in the space between, we are the told. Here we receive the gifts of being created and recreated. Of listening and wondering and crying and learning. Here we are characters. Myth. Legend. Here we can fly.

In a time before airplanes, before gliders, before balloons, and even before birds, a group of kids came through the door into the space between—into the invisible world where everything exists—before re-emerging back in the visible world to imagine flying into existence. Aren't you glad we did?

This is where we still come to imagine what's next. We come back to the gift we've had all along: the gift of deep imagination.

# Epilogue: my neighborhood wings

Despite initial worries, it was a simple act to regularly open our home to the whole community—to strangers—like Belit once did for me, I once did for Nicole, and now Nicole, Alex, Elyse, Isaac, and others do for others at our home in the CD. It was a small change for each of us to make. The courage we continue to gain together today—thanks to our connection to the space and to the place that holds us—isn't small at all. These lasting connections and courage regularly pull us out our doors and into the street to work and play with neighbors there too. Deep welcome, I call this now. This remembered ability to show up for neighbors in places and ways that work for them. Deep love of space and place are the gifts I receive from the CD and Collective Self. Deep words and gratitude and imagination are gifts from friends and neighbors. I carry these within me now. Move more fluidly as a result. I'll never stop giving back. I'll never stop being grateful.

Don't open your home as community space if you're not interested in being profoundly changed. Three years ago, I was a quiet researcher and blogger scared of inviting strangers in. Today, thanks to the constant stream of coworkers, friends, and neighbors, I'm the one who just keeps getting stranger. Now I'm the one who has to be reminded that there was a time when it didn't feel natural to deeply trust strangers on sight—both at home and in the street.

In September 2012, Chris deemed us—himself, a mama squirrel, and me—The Fucking Rescue Rangers! after we rescued four trapped, angry, hissing baby squirrels from a narrow, dark attic space and returned them, one by one over the course of a day, to their badass mom outside. I still keep a squirrel image on my wall as a reminder of mama squirrel awesomeness and human awesomeness.

In June 2013, after our space helped pull off the first (now annual neighborhood event) Hopscotch CD—with little more than neighbor-generosity, spit, and duct tape—fellow event creator, Knox, of Jackson Commons, knighted us Community Jedi Masters. He even gave us fancy green ribbons with Yoda on them. I keep my Yoda ribbon on the kitchen wall, so I never forget our Jedi status, the generosity of Knox, and that stories and titles offered to us as gifts from friends contain deeper magic than other stories and titles, including those I give myself.

Last year I was called a Leader in the Free Coworking Movement by Cat Johnson who interviewed me for a March 2014 Sharable article called "Free Coworking Growing Rapidly Fueled by Open Collaboration." Women all over this planet host work out of their homes every day. Turning a home into a community work space isn't new. We're all leaders here. I think this idea has just been forgotten as an option in some parts. Personally, I experience the space and place as leaders. See small groups and neighborhoods as leaders, not individuals. Then again, it feels pretty good to be recognized as a leader by a stranger—especially if you're often overlooked, like I am. I'm so short I can't even get people's attention at the deli counter until I jump up and down hollering and waving my arms. So thank you, Cat.

Nicole's been running the coworking space for more than a year now. I think of her as the Grand Pooh Bear of Coworking (like Grand Poobah, only even cuddlier and kinder). As Elyse takes over next month, Lord knows who she'll become.

A little over month ago—sitting next to Nicole and surrounded by the faces of new friends and old during coworking—I fully experienced the most fundamental part about creating and sustaining an in-home community coworking space and a thriving neighborhood: all we have to do is just keep showing up for each other, and keep remembering ourselves as vital community members, and magic happens.

I feel like I'm enough now. More than enough, actually. And so is everybody else here. If you take nothing else from this book, take that. We aren't just a struggling bunch of individual, frustrated, confused, scared humans anymore. We're family. We're community Jedi masters. We're artists and poets and game changers. We're the grand pooh bears of coworking. We're the 206. And we're the Fucking Rescue Rangers!

- Lori

March 5, 2015
written at The Pirate House on Whidbey Island, WA USA
(We're the 360 now, too.)

# Community Mementos

December 19, 2012

Dear Lou,

It has been a wonderful treat to spend time with you on your "work from home" days these past months. I have enjoyed the environment you create in your home with its spacious beauty, warmth and friendly critters! You are an important source of inspiration and connection with our local community. It is also just plain fun to be in your company.

Thank you for all that you share.

Setta

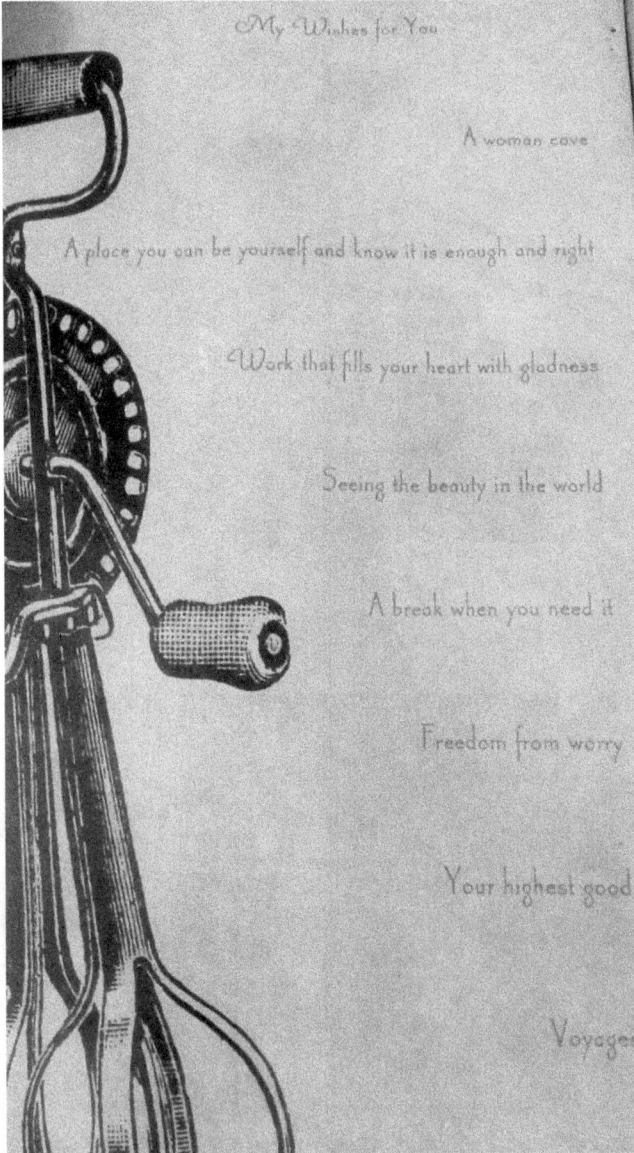

My Wishes for You

A woman cove

A place you can be yourself and know it is enough and right

Work that fills your heart with gladness

Seeing the beauty in the world

A break when you need it

Freedom from worry

Your highest good

Voyages

# About the Lived-Adventure Series

Recently I noticed that the books I'm writing are forming themselves into a lived-adventure series. Books are cool like that. I didn't plan this series (see Hint 67). I lived it. Many of the characters in this book, including me, can be found adventuring in other books too.

Books in the lived-adventure series so far:

1. *Different Work: Moving from I Should to I Love My Work* (2012)

2. *A Travel Guide for Transitions: Because Freaking Out About This by Myself Totally Sucks* (2013)

3. *Different Office: Stories from Self-Created, Soul-Satisfying Work Space* (2014)

4. *Year 1 Poet* (2014)

5. *Reimagination Station: Creating a Game-Changing In-Home Coworking Space* (2015)

# About the Author

Lori enjoys being created and recreated by Collective Self Coworking, friends, neighbors, and community. She loves the words wander, wonder, mystery, adventure, listening, creating, gardening, writing, poetry, chicken pirates, mermaids, and dragons. She's serious about home canning and collecting rocks and driftwood and seeds on walks: aspires to playfulness in all other things. Lori's especially interested in the fluid spaces between people and things—the foggy, messy, chaotic, dark, empty, lovely in-between places. She's currently petitioning the summer Olympics committee to get Extreme Neighboring added as a life sport.

Lori lives near Langley, Washington, USA with husband Daniel, Eva the dog, and Joe, Bella, and Batman the cats. To find more of her work, visit her Collective Self website at www.collectiveself.com, stop by for a chat on her Lori Kane, Author Facebook page, or follow her @CollectiveSelf on Twitter.

This photo was taken by Daniel Gregory. His work can be found on his website at www.danieljgregory.com.

# About the Cover Illustrators

The art for this book is found-object art. Nothing new was created for this book. These pieces were created as gifts by and for the community space in the past at some point.

Tabitha Borchardt, aka "Funkisockmunki" is a recovering graphic designer turned illustrator-weirdo who spends most of her time cultivating a garden, drawing, arranging sticks and rocks, and talking to trees and crows. She currently resides in the Pacific Northwest surrounded by as many plants and rainbow-emitting devices she can get her hands on.

Tabitha originally created the artwork on the cover for a Collective Self art show at Office Nomads in the spring of 2014. She then gifted the piece to Lori, who stares at it every day now. Tabitha is beyond awesome. Lori didn't remember herself as an artist until Tabitha showed up to make all the things together.

Thank you Tabitha.

Bas de Baar is a writer who draws. He loves to make visual maps and travel guides and card games for the collaborators of our brave new world. Bas lives in The Netherlands.

Bas originally created the artwork on the back cover of the paperback version of the book as a gift—a poster for the wall—for Collective Self Coworking in 2013. He just sent us an amazing poster for our wall across an ocean for the fun of it out of the kindness of his heart. Go team orange!

Lori didn't remember herself as an adventurer and chicken pirate until Bas showed up to co-pirate.

Thank you Bas.

Lori Kane

www.lorikane.com

www.ingramcontent.com/pod-product-compliance
Lightning Source LLC
Chambersburg PA
CBHW060509280326
41933CB00014B/2898